A PHILOSOPHICAL WAR

A PHILOSOPHICAL WAR

Part I:
Antebellum, Enemies, & Allies

JOSEPH ATMAN

Printed in the United States of America
First Printing: 2025

ISBN: 978-1-074233-56-3

Artwork by Enrico Salvadori
Cover design by Veronica Coello
Interior design by Amit Dey

Published by:
Planksip Press, an imprint of
SOMETHING OR OTHER PUBLISHING LLC
Brooklyn, Wisconsin 53521
For general inquiries: Info@SOOPLLC.com
For bulk orders: Orders@SOOPLLC.com

For Chuck & Anthony,

Finally, it's over.
We Won.

CONTENTS

CHAPTER I

ANTEBELLUM

THE INVISIBLE WAR

Although there are only a very few people who realize it, we are at war. It is a war that is so pervasive, so consuming, that we have come to think of it as a normal way of existing. This war, however, is not one fought by soldiers on a faraway battlefield; this is a war fought by all of us every day. But this is not a metaphorical war — far from it. What it is is a war more intense, more invasive, more dangerous, more real, and far more deadly than any fought by traditional means.

All war is conflict: war is the strategic and intentional struggle between forces in direct opposition with one another. War takes all shapes; it is inescapable in every society and has a ubiquitous presence at every moment of recorded history up to the present day. War is about territory, assets, and control. It is the most useful of all profit structures, the most oppressive of all aggressors, the most decisive of all arbitrators. War is the final factor. It is *the* determinant. When war is chosen it is the last act employed to reckon with opposition.

Many choose war as a means, fighting for some kind of strategic or political advantage: an opponent attacks another to gain land, or to consolidate power, or to garner resources. War is the product of dispute and serves as the terminal means of reconciliation. Of those for whom war is a choice, many fight for an idea. Many others fight to obtain something, or to ensure a way of life. While others fight simply because they were ordered to do so.

3

But there are other, far less ambitious, yet all the more dangerous soldiers. They are the children of war. They are guerrilla soldiers who wish for peace only to have had war thrusted upon them. Unlike their aggressors, these reluctant warriors can only fight or perish. Though, if they choose to fight, their struggles are the ones battled with the most heart, and often the most blood which it pumps.

We are in a similar kind of war: it is not one we have chosen, but one that has been foisted on us through the generations. In fact, we have never known anything but this struggle. And being so, we have never actually realized our situation as an ongoing conflict of choice, but rather complacently accepted it as an existentialism we must merely attempt to sift through as best we can.

And yet, the reality is that — for all intents and purposes — this war is a choiceless yet impassioned struggle that is of more danger and yet more consequence than any traditionally material war fought with weapons and armies.

This war is different.

This is not a war for land or for wealth. It is not a war over political ideology or religious belief.[1] Our war is different from other wars in the way the hydrogen molecule is different from the ocean: the ocean is immense, powerful, active, full of life. The molecule is isolated and small, delicate to change at a subatomic level; and yet, without it, water would not be. The hydrogen molecule fuels the ocean; though, they are not

---

[1] Despite what history might say, there has never been a war fought for religious reasons alone; regardless of what the declarations might site, all wars have some kind of political agenda behind them. The mere notion of a religion fighting another religion is absurd strictly based on the definition of what a religion, or religious ideology, is.

the same. And so it is with this war: without it, war itself as we have come to endure it would not be. It could not be.

But the problem is that few have opposed our aggressor — not because of a lack of will or strength, but because of a lack of recognition. The enemy, though ever-present, has managed to evade us completely. And yet, ironically enough, this war rages at every instance of our existence, oppressing, attacking, and destroying our very humanity. In fact, it is so oppressive, so exacting in its attacks, that we are not only unaware of its existence, but by our very actions we contribute to the strengthening of its assaults, allowing them safe passage and eventually harboring them without question. It is the most cunning tactical warfare ever crafted, and, being so, can boast to be the most powerful and the most effective. After all, all warfare is based on deception, and the best generals are the most insidious. With deception, weaknesses are drawn out of those deceived and the opponent strikes freely, overrunning targets that — because of the shrewdness of the siege — are overwhelmed completely.

And so it is with our war. Long ago the invading army delivered an illusory, near-fatal initial blow, and we were overrun before we even realized something was occurring — much less a full-scale invasion. It was a slaughter, biblically proportioned in its effectiveness and in its brash, unyielding mercilessness. It was a battle that was over almost as soon as it began: every kingdom fell, every division of opposition disarmed and dismembered, every civilian enslaved. And to this day, almost all of us still carry the banners sewn from our assailant's inglorious victory.

Fortunately, battles brought to one's doorstep are defended the most ferociously. But the cost is obvious: a tranquil home becomes a combat-zone. And in this, our war, the enemy has penetrated so deeply behind the lines of our territory that to extradite it will be an enormous undertaking that will call for the full arsenal of whatever weaponry we have against it. So, we begin to take up arms. But in our stockpiling we find another difficulty: our weapons, too, have been compromised; they exist, but in false-form — like toy guns beside impotent mortars. We have been under occupation for so long that what small weapons we do still possess have become relics of past eras — as if they were arrows shot at cannons, or chariots charging tanks. So, new weapons must be forged, and a new army raised and trained — one capable of not only fighting the enemy, but of dictating the terms of the fight with our newly formed armory.

The enemy is incredibly strong — overpoweringly so. It is so submerged, so deceptive, that its main tactic *is* submersion itself. And its deception is so great that we are not even aware that an invader is present. Furthermore, its attack has been delegated with such consistence that we are no longer cognizant of the offensive; its oppression has been quietly normalized and accepted as an inevitable way of life. In fact, we have combated it for so long that we have allowed it to become a part of us. And if it were suddenly to depart, we would feel orphaned by its leaving.

As it is with many soldiers returning home from battle, what they took part in becomes ingrained within them; the soldiers come home, but they are unable to shed the stench of violence from their olfactories. We see it all the time: a street-wandering former private begging for change on the corner, the maladjusted first sergeant who takes his own life. Violence is so forceful in its impressions that no matter how short the actual experience it resonates through a psyche for a lifetime unless properly managed. Violence is powerful, concise, and effective......And that is why it is so often used.

Unfortunately, this violence has become a part of us. The enemy attacks us aggressively, though, in silence, and we have become imbued with its onslaughts; and we are now so accustomed to these quiet acts of brutality that without them we would be unsure of ourselves. What's more is that — like a drug addict who has injected so much of the opiate into his body that to take the drug away from him would kill him — we, too, will die without our occupiers if they were suddenly stripped from us. We are so sickly infused with the poisons of our enemy that we would not even recognize ourselves without them. For we have become akin to an entire race of addicts teetering on the verge of overdose or faced with the painful death of withdraw. Our enemy is parasitic — a leech that sucks at our vitality. And we live shorter, weaker lives that are far less significant than they otherwise would be without the burden of this oppression.

However, there is an advantage we hold: the enemy's strength.[2] If we see that the enemy's greatest asset is that it gains its dominance over us by utilizing us, then we realize that we are the source of its power. A General is only as strong as his army and the utilization of the resources that army has conquered. And what's more: a general is only a general when he has an army, and an army is only an army — only a real power — in matters of war. If a thing's potential goes unutilized then it is powerless: a large rock and a small rock

---

[2] To dominate any conflict, one must turn the enemy's greatest strength into its weakness.

leverage the same amount of force while resting on the hillside; it is only when they begin to slide down the mountain that we see the difference in their force.

The same holds true in our war: the enemy is only strong because it opposes us, and it opposes us because it needs our cooperation to maintain the existence it enjoys. Our adversary's ruthless nature comes from its tenuous hold: what cannot survive on its own must continually scrounge from its host. This war *is* its existence. The addict and the drug are the same things; both need the relationship to function. Just as we would perish if we were to strip ourselves from the enemy, the same could be said of our aggressors: without us — without a thing to attack — they hold no power. And it is only because our persecutors have pursued us for so long that we have become ripe for feeding; we've been weakened, exhausted, starved-out and surrounded, and we've worn ourselves into the perfect prey. Like a master competing against a rookie, we have been precisely manipulated in an exact way: proxies, patsies, and stooges baited into maneuvers which seem like the right plays.

In the traditional wars we are familiar with, the war terminates when there is nothing left to conquer and no one left to capture, or when one or both sides have had enough of the other. But our war persists without a clear end in sight; for, again, it is the war itself that keeps our opponent alive. This being so, the enemy has reduced us to human batteries for their war machine. Again, our enemy exists *because* of this war: this war is the fabric of its being. So, it must keep us strong enough to live, yet too weak to fight back.

However, even though we have suffered defeats at nearly every battlefield we have entered up to this point, the dynamic we enjoy with our enemy gives us a subtle yet powerful advantage. Our secret weapon is that we have something our enemy does not: an existence outside of this conflict. Again, our opponent draws the source of its strength from keeping us embattled. But what if we refused to fight? Or, better yet, what if we obscured the battlefields so that there were no longer any grounds from which to attack? Our war will attempt to do exactly that: not so much combat the enemy by facing it head on, but more so alter the battlefield itself so completely that the kind of war our enemy seeks can no longer be fought. However, before we attempt this monumental reconfiguration, we need to come to a greater understanding of what it is we are battling for, and how the conflict began in the first place. Understanding these foundational elements will then allow us to finger the enemy itself, which we can then begin attacking directly while at the same time reorganizing the battlegrounds. So, again, we must ask ourselves, what is it that we fight? Why are we fighting it? And, furthermore, why has the battle come to our doorstep?

THE BATTLE OF BEING

In order to fully understand the breadth of what opposes us we need to comprehend some basic, though often overlooked catalysts of not only war itself, but of all phenomena.

At the onset, we need to recognize that while the law of motion which states that every action must have an equal and opposite reaction[3] might be quite sufficient for describing

---

[3] Newton's third law of motion states that every action must have an equal and opposite reaction.

how forces operate within the realm of physics, it doesn't go nearly far enough when speaking about the root workings of phenomena and Being themselves. Within Being (and subsequently what is perceived through phenomena) we must understand that for every action there is not only a reaction, but, more importantly, there is an *intention*; the action itself is merely a means. Intent lurks behind every act; it is the grand motivator of action.

Scientific observation asks the question "How?" Yet, one of the hopes of our philosophical war is to break through the veneer of the appearances of the physical world and go beyond them to obtain a true recognition of the structure of Being. And such a recognition is only obtainable by asking the question "Why?" It is a simple ask, and yet, ultimately, no branch of science can produce a viable answer. The scientific inquiry of "How?" is largely a question of mechanics. However, in "Why?" we open ourselves to the possible discovery of origin, means, and an ultimate direction of an act or thing. The same can be said our philosophical war, or any other: war itself is merely a means; it is never the final product or intention.

Similarly, in every battle there is an agenda which motivates it. Our struggle here is no different. As with all wartime clashes, it is fraught with intense and meaningful purpose if for no other reason than survival itself is at stake. However, the purposefulness of the fight that we are about to engage in originates from a cause far deeper than any cobbled together by paltry politics. Our struggle goes even beyond the mere fight for existence: *our war is for salvation itself*; it is for the very actuality of our own physical, mental — and, most importantly — spiritual being.

As we will show to be evident, this "spiritual" being is of the most paramount consequence to any individual regardless of one's theistic beliefs. And it is exactly because the struggle for salvation is at hand that the current existential human condition calls for the kind of war we are waging; in fact, it demands it. Our beings have been hollowed out by so many false-flag ideologies implanted within us by the moles of our enemies. But we long to be rejoined to something we cannot properly identify. And so, another purpose of the work within these pages is to not only identify that ineffable something, but to identify and then reconnect ourselves to that force which has long since escaped us. And, at its completion, our struggle will be one which delivers us into a kind of existential salvation that, if implemented correctly, will bring peace and perspective to those who seek it out.

RECONNECTING TO ORIGINALITY

Again, our current philosophical crisis is largely a fight for reconnection; it is a want to bring forth the originality of what it is to be a human being. As we will explore, our assaults will be generated from the premise that our modern being has, at the very least, been separated from its originality, and, in other, more extreme respects, that originality has been lost altogether. Humanity has apparently distanced itself from its sacred spirit; and now, in a feeble attempt to recapture it, we search for that spirit outside of ourselves in various forms of pleasure and what we think of as levels of success — which we believe will bring us joy, or, at base, a certain form of contentment. And all the while we search for something to connect to. The problem is, however, that even if we find that connection, we are unsure of how to actually do the business of joining together with such a thing; we find ourselves constantly at a degree removed from any true and meaningful linkage.

Whether it's due to a particular kind of cultivation from a cultural, financial, religious, political, educational, philosophical, temporal, experiential, or other kind of influence, we remain subjectively clouded by our own limitations and biases, which become hindrances in our ability to make possible that common bond we so desperately seek. And these biases hold us back from having an existence in which we have an actual, participatory connectivity to life in an unendingly meaningful way. Existentially, we no longer feel that we are ourselves — whatever we were in the first place. We are always searching. And what's more, within that search, often the only things we *do* discover are conflicts.

So, our counter-insurgence is fought in the hope that we might cease our incessant searching and provide for ourselves enough peace to utilize and enjoy the fullest extent of our beings. On scales grand and small, our mission takes root. And these opening pages are a mere guerilla attack at passing forces. However, the initial shots we fire at our enemy will point us to the possibility of something larger that we can eventually target. After all, most major conflicts begin as comparatively minor actions. Unfortunately for us, the vastness of the dilemma we confront here has festered due to the inattention we've paid to the smallest of details — details which have grown into monsters that we have come to accept as everyday occurrence or even the natural workings of a happening that has now grown beyond our control. Yet, these monsters that roam and wreak havoc on our humanity are not untamable; in fact, they are more susceptible to us than we are to them.

There is no doubt that under our current mode of being we are vulnerable to all kinds of existential and philosophical threats. Such threats are made possible by the way we have structured our consciousness and the subsequent lives that have sprung out of that conscientious construction. However, if we were to somehow change the way we went about the business of experiencing our consciousness, it would then be possible to have a new kind of human being altogether. It is a simple premise: changing our minds will change our way of being, which will alter the kind of beings we are.

Here, in our philosophical war, what we aim for is that new kind of being altogether — or, at the very least, we aim for a rejoining of the mode of what human being was in its originality. And with this new form of being we hope to gain an access to a direct participation with what we currently think of as actuality, reality, the way of life, or of what some might call the classical notion of God itself.

Life, after all, is a participation with itself; and we are an inextricable, intricate, powerful, beautiful, and vital piece of that participation. Yet, we have made that piece defenseless to its own misgivings. Through a lack of acceptance and an abundance of desire, we have created a want to become *more*. So, the question then arises: why is it that we want to *become* in the first place? What do we strive for and why? Anytime we wish to become, we seek-out something we hope to gain. So, what is it that we feel we have lost?

As we have already mentioned, it might be argued that our modern existential crisis arises from the possibility that we have lost our connectivity to something we can point to and call our own human nature: a reality that, while uniquely human, is also on a track headed towards a specific end. And if one accepts the notion that all action is born of intention, then a rather large difficulty hangs on the existential mantle: human beings have seemingly no ultimate intention whatsoever. However, as we will examine further, we might attribute this loss of direction to our endless search for meaning through our constant attempts at becoming — a becoming which is merely a notion propped up by human minds. Humanity's crisis is one of existence — a crisis of our relationship to Being, to reality, and, possibly most mysterious of all, to our own humanity itself. It is a crisis which attacks us from all angles, and not only are we incapable of fighting back because of a lack of proper defenses, but, as we shall soon explore, we are not even aware that we are being persecuted.

Though, we do feel the effects of this ongoing existential tragedy; in the modern world we often find ourselves isolated and alone. There is a pervasive theme to our lives which incites a frequency of fear, timidity, and an anxiety which leaves us utterly incomplete. We are in a continual mode of questioning our relationship to the world we inhabit. We search for metaphysical answers in the hopes that they might somehow serve to quell the dread of our prosaic encounters with reality.

At times, if the proper resolve is there, we turn our energies into one giant mission to 'find out' — a singular quest for meaning, or for any kind of feeling we can muster. But this process of 'finding' takes a great deal of attention and energy, and the task often overpowers the inquiry. So, because of the monumental nature of this process, we often take routes of lesser resistance. Such paths manifest themselves in various forms: we work jobs we despise, endure relationships with people we do not truly care for, conjure up acts we are not proud of — all because of an unnamable lack of will within us to do otherwise.

And these pathways, though easier to navigate than the alternatives, almost always lead us to deaden our spirits. We have become so anesthetized to these various experiences that we look for any kind of feeling we can extract from them, even in the forms of self-inflicted pain and suffering. We incur difficulties just to keep occupied, and embark on endeavors which further us from the truest natures of our spirit. All this we indulge in for a shot to merge with something purposeful so as to extract a tiny morsel of what our lives are meant for.

"WHY?" VS "HOW?"

Again, it is the deepest question we can ask: "Why?" And yet, because of institutional, cultural, or dogmatic systemizations, we most frequently engage in the far less consequential: "How?" But the "Why?" remains at the center of the mystery (or at least we have kept it there). In examining it further, what becomes all the more perplexing is that the question of "Why?" has usurped the importance of our attempts to connect with the inexpressible component of life which the question itself begs: there is a happening — and possibly, a presence — we cannot explain, but it is one which we nevertheless attempt to grasp in merely asking the question of "Why?" Through this asking, what we are really attempting is a kind of relationship *with*.[4] But *with* what? The question — and the subsequent, yet,

---

[4] The word "with" is used here intentionally and will come to have tremendous consequences as we move forward in our work.

incomplete answers we have produced thus far — have become more central to our attention than the actual importance of the happening or the potential presence itself. Yet, if it exists, this happening or presence is something in which we are indivisibly comerged with and surreptitiously yet profoundly influenced by.

And so, drunkenly unfashioned, our search continues; though, we are unsure of what it is that we search for, or what it is that we are asking; and further, we do not have we the cognitive, linguistic, or spiritual acumen to accurately seek it out if, in fact, we did. Though, we often fool ourselves. Again, we are not even sure of what it is we are asking, much less, how to ask. Even the simplicity of the question of "Why?" has varied interpretations as to what it portends. And what's more, as we have already recognized, the importance of "Why?" has been trumped by the wholly inferior query of "How?" "How?" begs at becoming: *How* do we get from one point to another? *How* does that work? *How* does this happen? *How* do we know? *How* do we *become* something more, something greater, something other than what we already *are?*

This is not to completely indict the limited, though often usefulness of the inquiry of "How?", but only to bring to the surface the fact that its utility has no bearing on the heart of the crisis we endure. And what's more, we generally only arrive at "Why?" after the details of "How?" have been realized as a secondary importance. The question of "Why?" usually happens only after "How?" becomes a worn-out instrument. Going further still, as we will find in the early stages of our struggle, language becomes insufficient when it comes to asking these types of questions in the first place. "How?" is easy: it is a mere recollection of a phenomenological happening. But "Why?" is a much more difficult investigation, so we frequently stray away from approaching it directly. And yet, partly because of its difficulty, and partly because we may simply be afraid to really explore it — or lack the proper tools in which to do so — the "Why?" always looms in the background of our processing minds.

In asking "Why?" we hope for a singular understanding — not *an* answer, but *the* answer. Answers are always the pursuit, and they often come in the form of a feeling or an experience we can take with us which gives us some resolve or peace. And from that resolve we obtain a better sense of ourselves and the general meaning of the occurrence — that is, we have a better sense of the "Why?", or, at least we feel we do. Moving beyond this, in the search for meaning we employ a hope, and in hope we find a kind of support which urges us onward. This hope is what fuels our curiosity, but it will also eventually come to extinguish it: ironically, if we found the true, absolute, and final meaning in a given thing there would be no more reason to interact with it; by our realization of it, the thing will have immediately served its purpose, and by doing so will have rendered itself simultaneously useless. If meaning were extracted and decided upon once and for all, the great questions would be answered. If meaning were finalized, all the sciences could stop their mad, void-filling pursuits of endless "Hows?" For, the "Hows?" would only be scenery. The institutions could fade away, and the beliefs, the dogmas, and all the other notions of "how" things are would all be forever disassembled, and we would simply exist without the need for further examination or pursuit.

Until then, however, we rely on the achievements tied to becoming. Though, at a deeper level, what we really rely on is hope. Even if that hope is falsely placed in the desire to become, it is still based on the innocence of a hope that we will ultimately merge with something consequential, lasting, and real, and through that merger we will find something more, something better, something just, or even ultimately something peaceful. Every action we take as a human being is either the search for that ultimate answer, or the active refusal to look for it. Either we ask all manners of questions about all manners of things, or we ask few if any questions and become complacent, and often dull along with it. Both roads lead us astray: if we question our lives it is because we feel disconnected from truth. And if we do not, should we take stock, we might find that we have merely accepted that the mere asking itself is hopeless in the first place. After all, if we were with truth there would be no reason to search for something more to become. On the other hand, in the asking we can also take refuge.

Yet, overall, our search for meaning and the elusive "Why?" has led us to become ever more remote. Like a frightened child who runs so far away that she no longer knows where she is, a new fear has emerged from humanity's original panic. Our bid to find meaning is one which ventures to locate ourselves in proximity to a truth we cannot define and can just barely glimpse. Of course, adding to our difficulties is the fact that whatever does catch our eyes is often greatly misconstrued.

We have many questions because we have many difficulties. And all the while we have distracted ourselves with amusements while living amongst the many horrors we have created, as if we were playing parlor games within a prison.

THE ECHO OF WHAT IS

If the picture we paint here seems melodramatic it is intentionally so due to the seriousness of the topic; and it is a seriousness that is compounded by the universal lack of an open discussion about our current existential state. Every philosophy, every science, every religion, and to a lesser degree, every culture and institution has made an attempt at the answer that we seek here. But because of some insufficiency in our approach or a shortcoming of our combative devices, all these various attempts have failed to penetrate the essential core of reality. So, the search — and with it the struggle — continues.

Like an army reduced to throwing the stones at their feet because of a dearth of ammunition, philosophically speaking, we've slung every conceivable kind of theoretical apparatus at our quest for truth, only to have them all miss their metaphysical targets. And instead of holding the lines at the places where we *have* made gains, we've retreated towards distractions and other less consequential time-killers. As a people, we sprint hand in hand to any kind of happening or bemusement which keeps us from having to confront the larger issues of our era. Sadly, in many instances, on scales large and small, our consciousness has simply decided to set its sights on things which serve it no purpose, thus, in effect, shutting it down completely. The light of reality has become too bright for our eyes, so we look only at the shadows on the wall, and from those shadows we make assertions about the light from which they emanate.[5] There are

---

[5] If Plato's cave comes to mind here the imagery is intentional.

a few who still squint to look — a few soldiers firing reserved bullets at a dim mark. But they are very few, for sure.

Really, at its core, only one true issue remains: attempts to obtain a purpose in life have failed us on scales large and small. Where we have an opportunity to see meaning, we see only functionality. Where we have the capacity to enrich our spirits, we lead ourselves towards the shiny objects of amusement. Where we have the chance to assert the power of our own unique natures, we fall back to the din of the hoard.

But just because our search for something more has come up empty does not mean that what we are after has no existence. We remain hopeful to come into the presence of meaning or to ignite an answer for ourselves, and to experience a kind of joining of forces between ourselves and our lives — to live in a harmonious relationship with creation and our full acceptance and acknowledgment of it — is to live in a state of *being with*. But because we are so far detached from the purity of this brand of existence — because we are so diluted by bias and false perceptions handed down to us through generations of misled thinking — we may not know meaning or understand the answer even if we were rejoined to it. The separation from *what is* — the distancing of ourselves from that which we truly are — has individually, societally, and globally, caused a great illness within us and within the world at large.

And so, humanity has remained sick for a long-long time. And we seemingly lie complacently within our own squalor, somewhere between bereft and catatonic; which is why the task in front of us is so mortally serious, and why the melodrama in these introductory pages runs so thick. If it weren't for this sickness there would be no need for philosophies, no need to search, and certainly no need to struggle. And in the absence of these difficulties a great comergence between humanity and that ineffable substance which surrounds all things would come to form, and a reconsolidation of a kind of direct participation with actuality would occur; this kind of happening is the great comergence humanity has sought through all its attempts to find truth or connection. It is the genuine and cooperative existence we strive for. It is the *"being with"*. And in such an exacting relation, meaning would not only be apparent, but ever-present. Humankind would be in continually crystalline dialogue with the entirety of reality, and not left clutching to brief, muffled encounters with the echoes of its whispers.

However, when we talk about the word "reality" we are not sure what it is that we speak of. Going further, even if we were to decide on a definition of the word, what reality is at its core is still something that not only are we unable to attain directly, but it is something that we cannot be completely aware of given the current construction of our general consciousness. When we seek reality out it eludes us. And when we attempt to speak about it we only distance ourselves from it. As our minds are currently structured, we are too influenced, too cultured, too identified, and too attached to even begin to approach the periphery of this ultimate something we refer to vaguely as that which ultimately *is*.

Because of humanity's natural innocence, we are susceptible to misinformation; and such susceptibility has led us to compose our consciousness in such a way that it is not only unable to attain what is ultimately real, but it often unintentionally leads us in the opposite direction of truth. However, reality, being as pervasive and all-encompassing as it is, shows us glimmers of itself that shine through the phenomenological cracks of the world. Yet, in most instances we don't possess the cerebral or soulful capacities to reach out and grab hold of what *is*; or, more accurately, because of all the barriers we have put between ourselves and reality, we don't possess the openness to let it grab hold of us — which, of course, is precisely where our problems start, and often where they end. Rather than choosing to fight for a relationship with *what is* as it is, we instead opt to distract ourselves with things that are seemingly more within our control.

And who could blame us? No person or thing has ever trained us to be able to commune with reality. All the religions, as beautiful as they may be at their cores, have now become dogmatic buffers between one's self and the truths they purport to espouse. All our modern education focuses on *how* things happen within the phenomenological field, but it seldom asks the student to participate in the business of solving the problems created by the very kind of thinking it advocates. And we now exhibit none of the defenses needed to ward off the political, economic, social, environmental, and personal difficulties we encounter daily; though, unfortunately, we are excellent at making them. In fact, both our thought processes and modes of being have become so backwards that the more problems we make for ourselves — the larger the distance we put between ourselves and reality — the more we feel like we've gotten somewhere or obtained something. Like a man who wanders into a maze, we become lost, deeper and deeper, turned around within the hedgerows of a labyrinth we ourselves have constructed. And because of this wandering we have fostered a great complacency that creeps up into every aspect of our lives. And yet, all the while the trials we have invented for ourselves become even more extreme — though we feel that we are at least relatively equipped to negotiate these difficulties.

What's more is that we are convinced that our path is a righteous one even though we can see turmoil in nearly every aspect of our lives. Although, there are many others in the modern era who do, in fact, feel that on both personal and broader levels we are prepared to maneuver through the many challenges that await us in the present time. With all sincerity, we place unmeasured amounts of faith into our social and technological advancements in the hopes that we might make gains thought to be impossible by previous generations. And yet, while on the surface these breakthroughs seem like strident achievements of an advancing and prosperous society, interestingly enough, no one seems to question why it is these so-called social, economic, governmental, or technological advancements are needed in the first place.

Usually when radical advancements are made, they are done so in response to a deficiency or an imbalance. That we are forced to continually strive *towards* something — that we are continually attempting to *become* — is a direct indication that there is something amiss within the way we go about the business of interacting both with our own being and the world in which we have created for ourselves through that being. One might say that we are sick, so our attempts at becoming are medicines which seek to cure that ailment. But the medicine has side effects. These medicines are like cats sent into a room to chase out the mice; soon enough, dogs need to be sent to catch the cats, and then wolves to catch the dogs, and so on and so forth.

The major difficulty, however, is that we are not even aware that the need for achievement, advancement, and overall becoming are not necessarily healthy signs of progress, but potential telltale symptoms of a major — possibly even terminal — illness. And what's more is that what we think of as vigorous, robust practices are the very things which keep us infected, as if we had lit a fire to fight a fire but have wound up only burning down the countryside. Exposing the process of how we have become ill is the first objective of our counterassault in this war. The second is to eradicate the disease. And in a third, final movement we shall lay the groundwork to ensure that such a sickness is never again a possibility.

Of course, no one seeks to struggle. We never look to any unnecessary challenge that does nothing to further our state. And there is no more joy in the realization of this crisis which is taking place within our own minds than there is in its public exposure: for, by indicting the consciousness we have built for ourselves over the generations, we begin to lay to waste a vast number of works done by many great people — most all of whom have carried out their efforts with good intention. But to struggle has become natural to our way of life; and to acknowledge this truth is an honest condemnation of ourselves as we presently are. But it is a condemnation because we believe that we are capable of something greater, something more, and something known already — though it is now buried deep within the ideological minefield of our own consciousness. It is a condemnation in the way a mother urges her child to do better because there is an unfulfilled potential within her. We know that, both as individuals and as a whole, we could conceivably attain a life devoid of the constant existential and philosophical strain we've encumbered upon ourselves. However, as things are currently, we have become both physiologically and psychologically sick, and that sickness has become a crisis — a crisis that starts within our consciousness yet affects the physical state of our bodies and the environments we inhabit. For this crisis is, at its core, a crisis of being; it is a crisis of who we are. And if we are not already in full crisis mode, the efforts of this war hope to bring us to such a state. After all, the more quickly we realize the crisis the more precisely it can be resolved.

THE STRUGGLE TO BE

Though, unfortunately, there are many who do not see humanity in its potential death throes, even though evidence of its abject sickness show itself at every level. However subvert, there is a sense that something watches us from the shadows, and its presence instills an anxiety about facets of our lives that should otherwise give us peace. This angst quietly taints our every act, spellbinding us into disregarding the fact that the notions we carry within us spill out to forge our beings; and, because of a mixture of hyper-inflated egos and the phenomenological misinterpretations ushered in by this quiet angst, our minds are brimmed with erroneous thoughts which bring forth an erroneous being in kind. And this combination spells ultimate doom for us both societally and individually. (Of course, we are not talking about an abstract society or person at a future time: we are talking about *this* society at *this* time — just as we are talking about both the reader and the author. Our conflict is so dire precisely because it is ongoing here and now; for it is as desperate as it is urgent.)

What this action calls for is not a reframing of the political, social, economic, religious, psychological, or scientific systems — all of which have had a hand in forming our current crisis. What it calls for is a complete destruction of the broader schemes of systemization itself. Systemization, left unchecked, almost always serves as a conduit of division; it separates and divides, opposing one against another. So, to combat this never-ending bipolarity, we have to reset our consciousness, detaching ourselves from the bias, from the preferences, from the identities, from the ideas, and from all of the things which — up to this point— have defined us, and, by doing so, have held us in stagnation.

Obviously, however, we must move forward and evolve. Yet, our preconditioning would have us believe that in order to move forward we must make a departure from our current selves; while, in actuality, nothing could be further from the truth. And although the commonplace thinking demands that we go and capture something 'out there' beyond ourselves, as we shall see, the real trick of evolution has everything to do with harnessing what is already present within. Put simply: we must cultivate a kind of *being with*, and not continue to advocate the current perpetual modes of *striving for* — modes which dominate our present ideology, not to mention our general praxis. After all, it is in the very act of striving that we abandon our present situation in the hopes of attaining something else. In the very movement *towards*, what we are doing is removing ourselves from an already existing situation and re-hitching it to some unknown state that we hope might improve our situation. Although, if we were able to see clearly, we would realize that the movement towards becoming is not the movement that contains the thing we ultimately seek — that ultimate connection with what actually *is* — which, up to this point, we have called "reality".[6]

And yet this is what our consciousness instructs us to do. It is what every dogma, every religion, every institution of every society, every psychological remedy and philosophical notion, every theory, every science, every system, every tradition in every culture wants to tell us how to *be*. All of which would be fine if it weren't for the undeniable fact that we already *are:* we are already connected — we are already what *is* — and yet we voluntarily seek to extract ourselves from that inherent worth and go off in a search to *become*.

So, we need to identify the want for this becoming, and from that identification we can properly extract it. Again, our sickness begins with a departure from the *being with* when we seek to become something we perceive as that which is different from what we already are. When we seek to change our original being, we look to gain sustenance from an exterior source; and in that departure we expend precious energy; and this energy expenditure is the root cause of our sickness. So, we can see clearly that this want *to be* is the true catalyst for our war.

Make no mistake: our war will be difficult and painful. But like a necessary surgical procedure, without it we will die; the consequences are literally that extreme. Because, like a virus, this sickness is one which will not stop until there is nothing left to feed on. So, we must combat it.

---

[6] We do not mean to say, however, that we should not attempt to progress as individuals or as a society. Yet, again, at the same time we must ask ourselves why it is that we need such progression in the first place......

WHY WE FIGHT

Outside of our objectives to identify the cause of our illness and then root it out, the third step in this process is one which is a task of the greatest imaginable importance. In a final act, the completion of our mission seeks to bring about a new being altogether — one which will bring an end to the need to reinvent one's self and one's society in the follied ways we have sought to do so in the past. This kind of being has been alluded to as "original being", or "pure being", or simply "Being" itself. As we go along, we will examine the fact that with all different types of Being there is something that exists that cannot be fully penetrated. And so it is with human being too: it also has its own originality — its own impenetrable space. And within human being that indefinable something exists no matter how frequently it is attacked, or by what measure. But, again, this kind of metamorphosis — this way back to our originality — can only occur once our sickness is removed. So, our aim is to extract that sickness; and the consequences of that removal are greater than we have come to expect for ourselves as a collective humanity, as a unified consciousness, and as a holistic spirit.

For, we have something our enemy cannot touch — a thing that this war is really all about: what we really *are*. After all, *this war is about what really is*. It is not a war for politics, or land, or resources: it is about survival. And we can live as we have been, or we can stand up and fight in this war that, though we may have enabled it, we did not consciously choose. This is a confrontation for a different kind of territory — a territory that only we as human beings occupy: the space of ourselves in which that unidentifiable originality of humanity dwells — that Eden within us. But that originality has been perverted, usurped, and obstructed by a vast and shadowy enemy. And the problem remains: we are so darkly aligned with what opposes us that its sudden extraction would bring down our entire way of being, save for that impenetrable space of originality within us.

For many of us, we have survived as prisoners under occupation: we have surrendered — which is not to say that we have given up — but we surrendered in the hopes that the army that will liberate us is on the march. So, pandering to our captors, we bide our time, existing as some low-brid mutation: a cross between our truest selves and what our occupiers have molded us to be. But, like any prisoner, we await our freedom, which, in our war is a reality that exists beyond the walls of our current reformatory. And to seek out this reality is not a want to become: it is a want to once again possess the freedom to *be*.

Of course, the main purpose of the counterattack we launch here is to liberate ourselves from the repression we have come under. And the first strike will be a place where our adversary is most vulnerable. But how does one attack something that has gone almost entirely unrecognized? How do we extrapolate ourselves from something that we are not only unaware is a danger to us, but something that we willingly, yet unsuspectingly harbor and feed? In fact, the war waged upon us is so subversive, so deceptive, we are not only unsuspecting of its existence, but we unknowingly do its bidding. Again, the best warfare *is* deception; and the more deceptive the better the tactic. So, if deception is the tactic, the tactic must be undone: it must be exposed. In any conflict, one must know one's enemy to truly combat it. So, that our enemy has operated under the veil of clandestance has thus far been one of its major strengths.

Our initial task, then, becomes a difficult one: identify the mole. We must first show that there is an invisible war taking place — a real war with real oppression — not just something drummed up by the author for mere performance and melodrama. We need to expose the ways and means of the opponent and demonstrate the necessity for our insurgence. And finally, we need to raise-up an army of our own — one which has been outfitted with the means and the motivation to retaliate, eradicate, and then occupy by thoroughly fortifying its position. After all, hearts and minds are won through proper motivation and proper fighting.

This war is an extremely important war, and although this portion of our project is written as a kind of performance, the stakes are every bit as high as those of the wars we have come to know, if not more so; the reason being is that if this war goes unfought then we are eternally bound to war itself. We are bound to a continual, unwinnable struggle which will consume every aspect of our lives — as it has in the past, and as it does so currently. This is a war against a singular, pervasive enemy of many faces and many powers.

It is an enemy that has been with us from the moment that Adam and Eve ate from the Tree of Knowledge;[7] in fact, this war is *precisely* what the God of the Old Testament attempted to keep us from before original sin condemned humanity to its eternal conflict. This war, our war — the one whose opening

---

[7] It is not, however, the author's intention to advocate for the authenticity of the accounts laid out in Genesis as historical happenings.

counter-shots are fired here — is the final war, and it is also the first. In fact, it is the only war that has ever truly been fought. It is a war whose enemy has, until now, been unexposed, yet has ruled over humanity as a puppeteer. And yet, here within our counter-offensive, we will not only kill off this puppet master, but by doing so we will carve a pathway for our reconnection to reality itself — a reality which has classically been termed as "God". In fact, at its highest point, what sets our work apart from most others is that when we see its successful completion, our war will make way for God's realized, actual return into humanity.

But this is not the god of religion or the god of theological pontification; it is the real, living ultimacy of an actuality we participate within at every moment. It is Being itself, but also what comes before and after it. It is not a god we have been taught about. In fact, the word "god" is so polluted in our minds that we will need to change the term altogether to understand exactly what it is we are speaking of here within the context of our war — for this is not the god passed down to us from history: it is the god of substantiality, the god of the present, the god of reality. It *is what is*. It is the connection to and the presence of the *being with*. And it is so far from what we have come to think of as the god given to us by the classical religions that after a short time we will no longer be able to even compare the old version of that god to the god we will introduce here. What's more is that our work will reinstate the capacity not for a messiah, but for the general form of messiahood. After all, once our war is fought to its successful termination, we will have no room and certainly no need for a messiah, or for a spiritual or institutional conduit of any kind; for, once reality is with us, we are more than nourished by it and it alone. In fact, we are given limitless life from reality here and now. And once we have a limitless life in the present, what need is there for the old notion of "God" given to us by religion?

This is not high-hyperbole. It is not some kind of allegory or fairytale drummed up for inspiration or to instill hope; reality is far more than inspiration and hope alone. Reality is limitless potential. But to see it, to *be with* it, we need to fight our way out of the sickness we endure; once we do that, we will have opened a space within ourselves, and in that space, we automatically gain a reconnection with actuality. And once we are unclouded by the forms of perception, we can go back to truth — back to an original mind capable of original thinking and sight. The removal of our sickness kenotically opens up a receptacle within our consciousness and our spirit for the ultimate reality — that which in the past has been called "God" — to come in to. That is what is at stake; because, without us realizing it, we are very sick, and it is this war that makes us so.

And the cause of that sickness, our enemy for several millennia, is *conceptualization*. Conceptualization delivers us from truth. Conceptualization brings with it nothing but misery in the forms of falsified ideology, abstracted thought, a want to become, depression, agony, suffering — all conflict itself. Every difficulty that has ever arisen, every problem of the human mind and spirit, every anguish, every torment, disagreement, clash, and war has been mothered by conceptualization. So, this is not a physical war in the way that armies gather together and fight; this is a war that if fought to a successful completion will end those types of transgressions. This is a philosophical war — a war of consciousness. And we are in it .... much more deeply than we know............

CHAPTER II

THE ENEMY

THE TREE OF CONCEPTION

RE-TELLING OUR HUMANITY

Before we go any further into our war we need to go back. And to fully understand how humanity became the kind of being it is presently, we must revisit a version of human history — even if it is not universally regarded. It should, however, be stated that not only is this version not universally regarded, it is not necessarily believed to be a historical fact even by some of those who belong to the tradition from which it emanates. Though, regardless of one's relationship to this version of history, we, nevertheless, need to reexamine the common narrative it gives us about the linkage between the kind of being humanity once had and the kind that it currently enjoys. And whether or not one regards this account as fact or fable, the historicity is not what we are attempting to debate. In fact, regardless of one's beliefs about the event, there is a great deal that can be gleaned from the mere moral alone; and for our purposes here it is really the mythos that is of the highest importance.

That having been said, we need to tell a story. Or, what is more accurate: we need to *retell* a story. It is a story we have all heard many times. In fact, it is one of the oldest stories known to humanity. However, we are going to put our own spin on it — one which should pull our war into a proper focus. But, again, we can hope that by retelling this story we might also come to an understanding of how our humanness took shape. After all, this is the story about how our world and our human being not only came to be, but, more importantly, why they both operate in the ways they do. Again, this is one of the oldest and most retold story of all time. Yet, for the purposes of our war, we will tell it in a nuanced way that few, if any, have done before.

GENESIS

This story begins as the great cosmic "once upon a time". However, unlike every other story ever told, this story begins, quite literally, with nothing. For, as this story goes, in the beginning, nothing was all there was; what is initially interesting is that at its very beginning this is a tale that predates time, space, and all occurrence itself. However, it is also the story of how time, space, and occurrences were born. Of course, there isn't much of a story if nothing exists, so, rather quickly, the story tells us that from nothing something came forth. (Most interpretations refer to this "something" as light, although the actual substance is more or less inconsequential.)

Interestingly enough, there is also a character introduced to us who is responsible for this initial happening. This character is central to the entire tale and all the subsequent happenings which stem from it, yet exactly who this character is remains a complete and utter mystery, even though, in the way the story is told, the character is spoken of as if the reader is innately familiar with its being. The character's title is the only thing we know about it and can identify; and that character's name is, of course, "God". Strangely, though, at least at the onset of the story, nothing whatsoever is said about who or what God is other than it created various things — beginning with "light". This mysterious God then swiftly divides the heavens and the earth and further manifests various forms of Being and the subsequent interplays of those beings. So, according to the story, God is really the principal motivator, the chief creator, and the alpha of Being. It is the great birth canal and the ultimate receptacle. And in accordance with this narrative, all things come into and sustain their being from God.

However, God, although very pleased with its creation, has a wish: it wishes to share its newly formed manifests with something it empathizes with, but also wants something to actualize and complete its creation. So, God decides to kenotically empty itself into another kind of being: human being. And from the idle Earth which it eventually inhabits, God forms the dirt in such a way that what was once dormant becomes animate.[8] This newly animated being shares many attributes with God. In this story, the commonly quoted line is that humanity was "made in God's own image".[9] This original being is then duplicated, and the two beings — famously known as Adam and Eve — are housed in an equally famous place: The Garden of Eden.[10]

---

[8] The Noological argument for God's existence states that, remarkably enough, all the requisite components for consciousness can be found within inanimate material that, once configured with a precise structure, gives rise to conscious beings. Also, it should be noted that the Hebrew word for "Adam" is very close to the Hebrew word for "Earth".

[9] Genesis 1:27

[10] The name Eden in Hebrew refers to a word roughly translated to "pleasure" or "delight". However, the more ancient Sumerian language from which the Hebrew translation may have come means something along the lines of "plain" or "simple".

In Eden, all is in harmony with all: there are no wants or needs, no difficulties or imbalances, no sicknesses or even death; being so, there was no need to become anything other than what one already was. There was a perfect, harmonious *being with*. In fact, everything was so perfectly on level with everything else, human being was able to communicate directly with God itself; there were no buffers or barriers between humankind and the ultimate source of all things. And this, above all, made The Garden of Eden what it was: the fertile ground where direct communion with God could take place.

Through this direct capacity to communicate, God lets it be known, quite clearly, that there is but one singular rule: there is a tree in the middle of The Garden that cannot be eaten from. Literally everything else is within bounds for humanity to participate with save for the fruit of the middle tree. However, in the legend, through the vehicle of the serpent — the sleekest of all beasts — Eve is tempted, and she, in turn, convinces Adam to also eat of the forbidden fruit.

It is interesting to note that Adam and Eve are not directed not to look at The Tree, nor are they disallowed to smell its flowers, or listen to its leaves, or even to touch it: they are ordered not to eat from it. If one was to take this as a strict metaphor (which is not necessarily what we are suggesting), this is a subtle, yet extremely significant move on the part of the author. After all, one can shut one's eyes or turn a nose or cover an ear, but once something is physically ingested it becomes a part of that person on a molecular level; the person and the food literally, physically become one thing. What's more is that the food is then converted into energy, and the kind of energy that is harvested is a direct result of the quality of what was swallowed. Therefore, we might deduce that whatever was consumed was something so extraordinarily potent that it had the capacity to alter an entire being, beginning and ending with Adam and Eve's consciousness.

And this is what happens at the middle tree — aptly named The Tree of Knowledge of Good and Evil: humanity is duped into relying on a sustenance that is forbidden by their creator. But why would God wish to keep Adam and Eve from the fruit? To answer this question, we need to examine what happened to Adam and Eve once they and whatever it was that they actually ate became one.

THE FALL

We know that once this fruit is ingested into their beings something immediately changes within Adam and Eve: they realize they are naked and discover a newfound emotion in shame; so, they clothe themselves — that is, they cover up their original, natural, and exposed being. Further still, in a pitiful turn of events, Adam and Eve come into another great and terrible new emotion that humanity has been attempting to shake ever since: fear. Adam and Eve were so afraid that the story tells us they hid. So, instead of roaming freely about as Eden's great caretakers as they were commissioned to do, Adam and Eve took up brief stints as fugitives of the one and only law set in front of them; and, understanding that something was amiss from having broken that law, they no longer felt comfortable to freely interact with their natural home. Of course, God — who was purported to have been walking through The Garden — finds them hiding and becomes immediately suspicious of their actions, and questions whether or not they had eaten from the tree. In a second, all-too-easy act, Adam exposes Eve's treachery to God[11] (once a sin is committed, sinning and other acts of self-servitude become extraordinarily easy actions to carry out, as humanity will spend the better part of its existence realizing), and God quickly susses out the fact that the covenant between itself and human being has been broken. The punishment is swift and final: banishment from Eden. After all, what has been ingested is final. There is no going back.

Life outside of The Garden is full of conflict: where before they simply worked with and within the happenings of Eden, Adam and Eve are now forced to labor within the world. There are difficulties at every turn; Adam and Eve's lives become a series of attempts to fulfil the newest aspect of their beings: wants — the largest of which is their desire to be someplace other than where they are, which, of course, is outside the gates of Eden. After all, not only are they subject to conflict and wrought with the need to achieve in order to have a peaceful existence, but outside of The Garden there lurks the ultimate enemy: death. Death was previously not something spoken of in The Garden, but beyond Eden's now impenetrable boundary,[12] death lurks as a mysterious and daunting undertaker which intertwines itself into every act and every shade of Being which Adam and Eve come up against.

So, this is the story as we know it: humanity is at peace in the world until they take a directive from a deceptive beast acting in the interest of undermining God's best laid efforts to

---

[11] Genesis, 3:12

[12] It is similarly interesting to note that Adam and Eve can never go back into Eden.

commune with its empathetic creation, and humanity becomes fallen — fallen from perfect being, fallen from its original self, and fallen from its creator and sustainer. Consequently, this happening has come to be known as "original sin" — the first offense and betrayal — and, theologically, has been termed "The Fall". Much has been written about this happening. Many religious and philosophical talks have been given on the subject, and entire religions and philosophies themselves have been spawn from these first missteps of humanity.

But, again, we, here at the onset of this war, are going to deviate slightly from the commonplace analyzations which have come before. Throughout the length of our war we will show that regardless of whether or not the happenings within Eden were actual historical events or a string of metaphorical allegories, something did, in fact, happen to us as human beings which, ever since, has kept us from being able to fully attain reality as it is; and because of that lack of capacity to harbor an unimpeded reality, it has had devastating consequences on the ways we have chosen to operate both as individuals and as a collective.

As unpopular as it may be in certain circles, we must also come to the realization that the story of The Fall *might* be just that — a story which does not have an evangelical or historical backbone. On the other hand, however, we must further acknowledge that, regardless of its historical accuracy, it is the meaning *of* the story itself which holds all true and lasting consequence. In fact, the creation story — along with many others from various sacred religious texts — may be even *more* powerful as a metaphor. Regardless of the story actually having played out with material characters in the way it is described, there is plenty of relevant truth within it.

HUMANITY'S GRACEFUL DANCE
WITH CONFLICT & DEATH

At its core, the story of Adam and Eve's banishment from The Garden is the story of why we encounter and live with sin — sin which brings about conflict, difficulty, and moves us away from the saving powers of the grace of the biblical figurehead known as "God". Regardless of one's religious beliefs, we can all look out objectively at the world and see that there are many chaotic happenings within it — most of which are caused by a certain mode of humanity's own being. There is a pervasively clunky dance humanity does with the otherness it encounters; and although it is impossible to encapsulate the entirety of the imbalance, it nevertheless rears itself in the unfoldings of everyday occurrences. This is evident in many facets of our lives — on scales large and small — from the constant conflicts which materialize in wars, poverty, famine, disease, and other worldly horrors, to the minutiae of our ready-to-hand lives that manifest as any number of discontents about the general direction of our individual beings and the unrealized purpose and meaning within them. One might argue that it is because of this unrealized purpose and meaning of our lives that we have spun the world into such a chaotic twist. And then, at the end of all this misery and conflict we cause and subsequently endure, the only thing that we are assured to gain is the prospect of death.

Of course, what death *is* can be debated. But we would lobby that death is of far greater consequence than something physical merely ceasing to be; in fact, one can easily understand that while a person or thing might be physically alive, at the same time, such a person or thing might exude such a lack of vibrance or affect that its existence could be regarded as death's equal. For, death — at its most basic and its most dangerous — is a mere state; and it is exactly the state our enemy is pursuing for us. In war, one's enemies are out for one of two things from their opponents: their surrender or their destruction (both of which generally yield the same result). Our enemy in this war has thus far achieved the former, but its occupation will surely lead to a real and true death far beyond that of something which exists as a mere physical state. And this is what we are in fact up against: real and actual death — which is why it is crucial that the story of The Garden of Eden and our counter attack be taken so seriously. We would argue that death, *immaterial of the existence of an afterlife*, is something that can happen to any soul. And death — the true and real death that our enemy seeks for us — is so final and so real that once it has been achieved there is no record *of* or subsequent effect emanating *from* the thing that was. This death (again, *immaterial of the existence of any kind of being beyond this world*) is the end of Being itself — both physically and metaphysically. So that is what we are up against: we are up against death itself — the ending of all Being and Consciousness.

And although The Garden of Eden sets up the framework for The Fall, it also sets us up for a glorious return to it — which would be death's polar opposite: life! But this would not be just any life: it would be a life that we have sought ever since that fruit was taken into our beings. So, let us take a closer look at what it was that really went on within the confines of those holy gates, and explore how, within humanity's extraction from Eden, that banishment also sowed the seeds for our eventual return.

IDEA AS SIN

Again, it cannot be overstated that whatever happened when Adam and Eve ate of the fruit from The Tree of Knowledge of Good and Evil, it disconnected them from the harmony with the world that they had previously enjoyed. Before Eve's encounter with the serpent, all is peaceful in both The Garden and the lives of the humanity who dwelt within it. But upon meeting the serpent, *even before the fruit is ingested*, something happens: the serpent implants an *idea* within Eve's mind. Whether taken as fact or fable, this happening points to what may have well been the first actual idea ever thought by humankind. And it is an idea that takes the form of *doubt*.

Again, whether or not the encounter with the serpent actually took place is immaterial; what *is* of major consequence, however, is that before an abstracted thought was placed into the mind of (a) human being, all was harmonious. Furthermore, that the idea took the form of doubt is equally important: after all, Eve had never previously questioned whether or not God's only law should be obeyed. The eating of the fruit was not a temptation until the snake puts a *notion* into Eve's head that doing so could be to her benefit — a notion that leads Eve into the doubtful cavern that she, along with the rest of humanity, will inhabit from then on. Doubt is significant because of its utility: doubt leads to questioning something given or apparent, which, in this case, is human being's relationship with creation. However, as soon as doubt arises there is a rift within humanity's consciousness and the so-called paradise they had, up to that point, enjoyed; in fact, Eden is looked upon as being potentially second-rate in light of what could be.

The notion that there could be more *is* Eve's temptation; of course, the potentiality that something else exists is a want to *become* — which is a seed grow from doubt's fertile soils. Again, before doubt arouse within Eve there was a kind of pure being that coexisted between humanity and The Garden. And in that purity of existence there would have been no need for doubt, or its mother: abstract thought. According to the legend, it is the serpent that introduced all of humankind to the tool that our war seeks to overthrow and restructure. However, this tool is one we rely on more than any in the modern world: it is the process of thought itself.

A NEW ARMY OF THINKERS

Now, we must be very clear in stating that our war does not seek an army of non-thinking soldiers — quite the opposite: what we wish to cultivate is legion after legion of well-armed warriors who are not handcuffed by the devolving thought processes that have been in decline ever since Eve's encounter with the serpent (ad nauseam, whether such an encounter was metaphorical or not). We hope to organically grow a battle-force that does not blindly follow the patterns set up and handed down by the previous generations. The army we aspire to will be constituted by those of a consciousness devoid of the thought structures which have spawn all hardship, dualism, and the endless wants put forth by millennia of doubtful-mindedness. For it is only when disharmony is present that the kind of thinking which led to Adam and Eve's banishment from Eden trumps the existence they enjoyed previously. As we shall see, if there exists a harmonious relationship between any two things, the need for abstract thought becomes completely and utterly moot.

POSTULATING A LACK OF NEED FOR ABSTRACT THINKING WITHIN PRIMITIVE HUMANITY

One can imagine that in a world where everything existed in a completed symbiotic relationship with everything else, the need for the kinds of ideas produced by abstract thought would be unnecessary; in that kind of world, human beings — along with all other things — would have enjoyed a relationship which so connected them to their environment that they would have been altogether inseparable and even indistinguishable from it. Therefore, it's wholly unsurprising that the environment depicted in Eden is described as one where Being and the individuals observing that Being operated together in a unified movement; being so, the kind of abstract thought implanted into Eve's mind would not have had much utility before her encounter with the serpent. For, in unity we find only simple Being interacting with other Being; but when encountering division, we experience the need for a kind of consciousness which can go about the task of reunifying that which needs mending. And the task of reunification demands the kind of mind which is capable of analyzing, comparing, and abstracting; however, this is not the type of mind Adam and Eve are described to have had.

After all, what need would there have been for abstract thought when one's existence and purpose were defined and furthered by one's own individual being and the interaction it had within the grander realm of Being itself? In any relation where multiple entities comprise one another there is little to think about: the union formed through the relation of the various entities creates a certain kind of being that is substantiated and given purpose by and through the created happening; humanity's present lack of this connection is directly responsible for the broad-sweeping existential crises it finds itself mired within here in the modern era. Without this direct connection with the kind of original Being described in Eden, humanity has become the only being within the pantheon of the observable universe that is unsure of its purpose and remains generally at odds with its environ. And this lack of direction has caused a great divide in our spirit. So, the question must be asked: how did we become estranged from our inherent mission and purpose?[13] For, as the legend of The Garden of Eden indicates, ever since our estrangement from paradise we have been made to continually wander the Earth in search of something which fulfills our lives through meaning and resolve.

Delving further into the workings of our own human minds, we need to understand that ideas themselves are not necessarily the products of consciousness; which is to say that one can be without giving birth to an idea. And although we may think of Adam and Eve — or any kind of primeval humanity — to have possessed minds with similar *capacities* to those we observe within ourselves in the modern day, we might also be served well by realizing that primitive humanity

---

[13] This assumes that we had an initial purpose in the first place. Of course, our purpose could, in fact, ultimately be to extract meaning from and give meaning to.

had a drastically different relationship to its surrounding; being so, the consciousness of early humans would have naturally been structured in modes which varied significantly from the forms we currently enjoy. And one of those significantly varied forms may have been the lack of a need for abstract thinking; that is to say that the need for ideas in the ways in which we currently implement them may not have been in existence because their utility would not only have been unnecessary, but ideas themselves may have actually been harmful to the kinds of being humanity possessed at the time.

THE SYNTHESIS OF THE ABSTRACTED MIND & ITS SUBSEQUENT CONTENT

Thoughts and ideas need a certain kind of consciousness in order to be produced. This consciousness is often termed a "mind". Here it is useful to imagine the mind as a kind of container, and thoughts themselves as objects within that container. And while the mind is the receptacle and activator of thinking, ideas are always thoughts *about* something; and, endemically, thoughts must contain content. However, the process of thinking involves an individual consciousness to receive or produce a thought itself, which immediately sparks a blurry relationship between the thinker and the content of the thought. The connection is obscure because although thoughts and ideas need a mind to sustain them, thoughts are not the mind itself, but only a portion of what the mind contains. So, we might say that when a mind encounters or creates a thought, the thought is something which is both a part of and yet separate from the mind in which it exists; that is, the singular thought is not the mind, but it can influence how the mind operates, just as the operation of the mind might influence the way a thought is received or produced. Going further, thoughts can be shared, while a mind is more personalized to a very particular amalgamate of thoughts and experiences, and is impossible to share in full — even with itself.

However, it should be noted that the mind and its content often serve to compose and influence one another until the two are so commingled that they become indistinguishable from one another.[14] That is to say that the mind becomes the content of its thoughts and the thoughts come to compose the structure and elasticity of the mind. Therefore, if a mind is structured in a certain way it can produce and house certain kinds of thoughts; and in a similar fashion, if certain thoughts are impressed upon the mind, that mind will be altered because of them. However, even though both the mind and its content come together to compose one another, each may still have different origins and existences: a mind can still exist without a particular thought, just as a thought may enter into a mind that was previously unaware of it or even unable to receive it. Given this, we can see how the mind and the object of its thoughts can operate simultaneously as two different actions.

---

[14] Often it is said in Eastern philosophies that one needs to learn to jettison his or her thoughts so that one's mind is kept open and clean. The point being that the observer is only able to truly obtain reality when thoughts and preconceptions do not interfere with one's ability to encounter what is.

For example, if one was to think about X, the thought of X would be housed in the mind of the thinker. Of course, it is of the utmost importance that we see that the thought *about* X is different from the reality *of* X itself. However, the thinker and the content of her thought (X) have a relationship made possible by the mind of the thinker. Being so, the thought of X is housed within the mind of the thinker and creates a relationship between X and the thinker that can affect each other's being. If the thinker conceives of X and believes it to be a certain way, this belief will affect how she might interact with X if she were to encounter it, and that interaction may in some way alter the actual being of X. And yet, although the physical or metaphysical being of X itself may be contained elsewhere, the thinker's being is influenced by the content of her thoughts about X. So, we see that thoughts are both separate *from* and a part *of* the thinker at the same time. But, again, the thought *of* a thing is not the thing itself; the thought will always be skewed by the thinker's limited perception and comprehension. So, the trick is to do away with the thought and interact entirely with the reality (of the thing). However, in a mind that has become entirely composed of thoughts, leaving those thoughts behind in favor of the unabated reality (of a thing) can be a near impossible undertaking.

THE CONTENT OF CONSCIOUSNESS PRODUCES THE INDIVIDUAL BEING & VICE VERSA

To begin following the bread trail through the labyrinth that is the relationship between Being and Consciousness we must perform a kind of thought experiment on ourselves. Some might find it a difficult experiment precisely because we as human beings *do* have very prominent egos and individualities. However, to comprehend the upcoming notion, the reader must pretend that he or she is without an individual being, but exists as Consciousness in a pure, grand form — a field and action untethered to any individuality, but existing in a thoroughgoing plane of observation.

As individual beings, we are constantly in a myriad of different states of various kinds — whether they be emotional, physical, or psychological; but all these states are linked back to ourselves as individual beings. When something happens to or occurs within the individual self, whether or not we recognize it, we process that happening through our beings and it comes to influence us in a particular way. Some events have major consequences on our beings, others are so miniscule that we never recognize them at all. However, if we were able to detach the consciousness[15] of our individual beings and transcend it into Consciousness as a grand form, what would we then come to realize?

The first thing we might become cognizant of is that Consciousness is the simple awareness *of.* Without the hindrance of an attachment to an individual being, we can see that, in its larger form, Consciousness is merely the act of passively recognizing a being, thought, or occurrence. Of course, consciousness is commonly thought of as belonging *to* an individual; however (although neither way of looking at

---

[15] The usage of lower and upper case "c" is intentional: the lowercase "c" is linked more to an individual being that possesses consciousness, while an uppercase "C" is used when referring to Consciousness as a grand form or field in its totality. The two words "consciousness" and "Consciousness" may as well be two different ones altogether.

it is completely precise), it might be more accurate to say that Consciousness has beings rather than to say that beings have consciousness; to understand what is meant by this we must briefly delve into how beings and Consciousness relate to and create one another.[16]

THE CONTENT OF CONSCIOUSNESS PRODUCES THE INDIVIDUAL BEING & VICE VERSA II: CONSCIOUSNESS & ITS CONTENT

Whatever Consciousness is aware of is its content. Content is anything recognized by Consciousness. So, when individualized being or consciousness takes place, what is happening is that there is an awareness *of* a particular thing *by* a particular thing. But the particular thing is only created when the grand form of Consciousness clings to and segregates the content it takes in; that segregation inevitably comes to form what we know of as an "individual" being or occurrence which exists within the larger field of Consciousness itself. That is, once the content that arises within the field of Consciousness is identified with distinction, that newly-minted distinctive notion, act, or general recognition becomes an individual thing in and of itself precisely because it has been identified as such by Consciousness; this identification effectively transmutates Consciousness from a *field* (or grand form) into an *individual* being by emptying into a particular, distinctive being. That

---

[16] A great deal more will be said about Consciousness and its relationship to Being and vice versa in the chapter "Vim, Verity, and Consciousness".

kenotic emptying of Consciousness as a form to consciousness as an individual being or occurrence happens on both the physical and metaphysical levels — creating both metaphysical thought and physical being with the same kind of process; and although this may sound to some like a glossing over of several very fundamental assumptions about the nature of the creation of Being itself, at its simplest level all that we are acknowledging here is that the conscious individual participates in the grand form of Consciousness where he is recognized by both his own consciousness and Consciousness in general (whether it be in pure form or in the conscious operations of others) as having an independent existence precisely because both the grand form of Consciousness and his own particularized consciousness view himself as an individual, independent being.

So, by sorting through its content, Consciousness comes to split and then restructure itself as a variety of individual beings that stand out against one another through this very sorting process itself. Similarly, once an individual thing gains independent being, that individual immediately acts on the consciousness contained within it, which, of course, is composed of content. Together with its consciousness and the content therein, the individual goes on to refine the relationships it has with its content. This refinement can also serve to create new content; so-called "new" content — much like the "old" — takes the forms of distinctive thoughts and beings, and the intertwining of these acts come to then doubly reflect in the individual being; that is to say that the individual consciousness and its particular content then go on to not only influence but actually *create* other beings and consciousnesses by the very process of its capacity to distinguish and segregate its content; and that distinguished content then creates and encounters other beings and consciousnesses and interacts with them by influencing and implementing the content within their own consciousnesses, thus evoking a chain reaction of individual consciousness gaining their independence. Therefore, the content of one consciousness influences and creates not only the being it is housed within, but other beings and consciousnesses and vice versa.

IN PURE OBSERVATION DEVOID OF THOUGHT, THE OBSERVER BECOMES THE OBSERVED

Here it must be further articulated that the thought is different than the reality. No matter how accurate such a thought might be, thoughts are abstractions, and abstractions are merely reflections on realities. So, while a thought may closely align with a reality, such a thought is nevertheless an abstracted reflection *about* a particular thing, but the thought of a particular thing is not necessarily the way such a thing actually *is*.

In order for an abstracted thought to have the best chance at lining up with reality, the thinker — to the best of her ability — must remove her own self from the process of the myopic and individualized consciousness and — again, to the best of her abilities — join herself with Consciousness in its grand form; that is, in order to have a thought commensurate with the reality of a given thing, one must participate in a state of pure observation which can only be obtained by surrendering one's own egoic perceptions, bias, and limited capacities — all of which routinely obstruct the ability for clear comprehension. Of course, in further irony, this process is no longer what we refer to as "thinking", per se, but is entirely more in line with what we know of as "action". Further, what a "self" or a conscious individual actually *is* is a collection of both mental and physical conscious recollections and current viewpoints that come together to form a perception about phenomena itself, which it then, in a quasi-false move, deems as "Otherness" — thus, setting up a distinction which simultaneously gives rise to a "self" (or vice versa). Circling back, for an individual to have a thought *about* a thing, that individual must bring other thoughts or experiences into its own individualized thought process. But in pure observation, the observer and that which is observed become undistinguished precisely because one needs the other in order to be, and both exist by virtue of the same act: one is the action (content), the other the observer (Consciousness).

So, again, what is extremely important to recognize is that when the comprehension *of* or interaction *with* a given thing is perfectly aligned with reality, there is no need or even room for what we currently conceive of as thought. Clear comprehension about a given thing eliminates the relationship between the observer and the observed and combines the two into a singular happening where that which is observing and that which is being observed become the same process. That is, consciousness in its particular, individualized being melds with the grand objective form of Consciousness, and the "individual" and the thing observed cease to have a distinctive existence, but are unified within the grand form of Consciousness; for the grand form of Consciousness is that which holds all content and unifies it, yet it also gives rise to the distinctive individual; therefore, when the individual observes purely — without the impeding bias of her own content — she relinquishes her own perspective in favor of the unbiased perspective of Consciousness's grand form. So, when a mind comprehends or observes a thing purely — or, without the interruption of the contents of its thoughts or experiences — thinking becomes an unnecessary and even obstructive process. Put simply, when the self-aware ego of the observer does the business of pure observation, the consciousness *of* a given thing is just that; where, exactly, the consciousness emanates from becomes of little consequence. Both the observer and that which is observed manifest and sustain one another, and the space saved for abstract thought within the individualized consciousness is lost to the far superior process of pure being through fully conscious observation. Furthermore, the clarity obtained through this egoless "thought" process turns out not to be thinking whatsoever, but rather, as mentioned, unobstructed observation — or what some might call unfettered perception or a capacity to see what *is*.

THE MIND'S ANCIENT OPERATIONAL CHOICE

In any relationship there exists a connection beyond the realm of analytical thought. Relations of every variety and the connections they produce have a pure being within the larger frame of phenomena, and when consciousness is introduced within this pure being there is only observation *of*, not ideas *about*. For, in their true essence, ideas are really the products of something altogether more subjective and even selfish. The biblical serpent that first appears in Genesis illustrates this perfectly: when the snake encounters Eve it impresses a viewpoint on her which she hadn't previously held. From this newly formed vantage of Eve's own being, an idea emanates from her now hyper self-aware mind. As humans, now many generations removed from those initial thought processes laid out by primeval man, we realize that it is from this awareness of our own beings that we immediately recognize a disconnection with phenomena at large; we, as individuals, oppose the greater forces of the world — that insurmountable otherness which leans on us at every instant. This realization calls on us to necessarily act out against this grand and constant opposition that our abstracted minds have dubbed as something which needs to be opposed and conquered in order to thrive within. Because we have conditioned our minds through the ages to see ourselves as disconnected, we have orchestrated those same minds in such ways that they have set themselves to the task of attempting to reconcile their own existences within the world.

And yet, in opposition to the analytical, problem-solving minds we have cultivated for so many years, we may be better off setting our minds to the task of mere observation. A consciousness geared towards pure observation will act in direct accordance with that which it observes and not from any ideas generated *about* a given thing or set of circumstances, as we do in analytical thinking. Yet, this approach of merely observing and then acting upon those observations is not the path that our modern minds have chosen. We have opted to follow abstract thought and the egocentric derivatives which come from it — namely in the forms of idea. After all, in order to have an idea *about* something one must see one's self as separate from the object or content of one's thought; this is precisely how our common era minds process existence: we see ourselves as wholly independent individuals up against a litany of events that may otherwise damage our beings or even bring about our ultimate demise. This viewpoint leaves little room to go about the business of observation — a happening which might otherwise allow for us to connect more deeply and harmoniously with our immediate environment. And, in such a connectivity, thought, in its current utility, would not be as necessary for our consciousness as it is in the way that it is currently constructed.

THE IRRELEVANCE OF ABSTRACT THOUGHT

Of course, we seldom take the time to observe the utility of our own thoughts, much less, how thought works as a process. Thought is the product of a self-aware consciousness that interacts with either its own content or what it deems as "Otherness" in order to analyze, project, or problem solve. The difficulty, however, is that thought fractures both the being of the thinker and the relationship the thinker has with reality; for, thought operates at a degree removed from reality given that the thinker must conjure up a newly-created metaphysical space in order to produce thought in the first place; which is to say that when thinking occurs, it is done so apart from the thinker's relationship to exterior objectivity and unfolds on a plane created and sustained by the thinker himself. Furthermore, thought must have an object, and objects are limited in both scope and form, causing thought to follow suit. Given these factors, there is no way to gain a lasting relationship with reality in its totality by relying on thought alone, since the objects of thought will always be limited by their own being; this being so, any limited form or event cannot present the observer with a wholistic picture of reality, but can only give the observer morsels of incomplete truths — especially if the observer's consciousness leans heavily on thought as a process.

So far as the thinker is concerned, again, when thought occurs, the thinker's being also becomes fragmented; while involved with thought at nearly any depth, the thinker, to a certain degree, loses touch with her physical existence and creates another metaphysical reality, however brief, around the object of the thought.[17] That being the case, when thinking occurs, a subsistence in both the physical world and a newly-crafted metaphysical plane is simultaneously maintained by the thinker. And as any thinker can attest, it is not unusual for one who is deep in thought to be wholly unaware of anything else going on around him in both the physical world or within his metaphysical consciousness. For, in thought, one loses one's full capacities for observation; the thinker is always tainted by the thought, and, what's entirely more dangerous, by what the thinker believes he has understood because of it.

However efficient human beings have become at abstract thought, it still might be difficult for us to comprehend the fact that in any kind of being which operates in harmony with another existence or reality, ideas become inconsequential, and thus, generally useless.[18] We see evidence of this thought-free comergence where relationships amongst particular beings or elements are composed of action alone. And, again, where there

---

[17] It is important to note that "reality" here is an all-inclusive combination of both physical and metaphysical space. Obviously, any definition of "reality" that excluded any portion of existence would be incomplete at best.

[18] Of course, ironically enough, the art of thinking is done through the process of abstraction (or vice versa); or, in other words, thought itself is a process of abstraction that arrives at another abstraction.

is pure action, abstract thought is wholly unrequired; in fact, we might even imagine how abstract thought would become an impediment in a relationship based purely on interaction. For example, in the creation of water, hydrogen and oxygen do not think about the consequences or potentialities of their union: they simply bond, interact, and be. Of course, elements of this nature are inanimate; however, it could be argued that their "inanimate" nature is by design (or, at the very least, default), as hydrogen and oxygen do not need to possess complicated minds in order to attain their functionality.

Even in the animal kingdom (and often in the human fiefdom) there appears to be little thought involved in finding a mate or defending a territory, or with any number of other primal pursuits; and this is not to say that choice is nonexistent in the natural world, but more so that there exists only simple action in, of, and for itself; and when the best possible opportunity is presented, such an opportunity is eventually acted upon to the furthest reaches and capacity of the being(s) involved.

In actions between two or more entities that compose one another and complete the other's functionality, the reality and utility of those various beings becomes evident, and they operate together in a pure and unified function. And, again, through the interaction of pure functionality — that is, in pure action in and of itself — thinking is an unnecessary occurrence. After all, the conceptualized, analytical minds we, as human beings, possess, must ask the question: *why is there thought in the first place?* Here, the word "thought" does not mean "consciousness"; things can be "conscious" without "thoughts" as we as modern-day human beings have come to experience and utilize them. Thoughts or abstracted ideas often have almost nothing to do with the grander reality that exists outside of them. Abstracted thought alone cannot alter external occurrence without a corresponding act which takes place within the realm of Being; that is to say that no thought alone is influential without a certain degree of action backing it. To be truly influential beyond the metaphysical realm, one has to introduce action or praxis into Being; and in order to have true and real change within Consciousness, phenomena, or Being, such a movement must be made with one's whole individualized being so that the phenomenological actions influence the metaphysical realms of thought, and those abstract spaces within a consciousness, in turn, influence the physical happenings that surround it.

Once again, we see this lack of the need for ideas most obviously in the animal kingdom: although animals are clearly conscious and have emotions and various forms of thoughts, they do not appear to do the business of abstract thinking. However, this is not to say that animals are *unable* to think abstractly — as, for example, there have been a number of documented cases where certain primates have been taught sign language and seem to be able to communicate abstract ideas with human beings through making gestures and symbols with their hands.[19] In a more relatable happening, many pets seem to have a capacity for what we think of as "love" by their overt affection for and loyalty to their owners. However, the breed of "love" and affection generated from the animal is one of pure action and is only abstracted by a conceptualized mind underwritten by thought as a process; which is to say that what

---

[19] Though, we should realize that those animals are using a tool humanity created through abstraction which was then passed on to a capable mind with an opposable thumb.

might be interpreted by the abstracting mind of the human owner as "love" is but pure, unadulterated, surrendering action on the part of the pet — and such action exists beyond the limits of abstraction; for, to abstract the act and parade it around within the conceptualized thought process somehow defiles and strips it of said purity.

Truly, abstract thought is the curse and luxury of the consciousness displaced from the rest of Being. But this only goes to show that in a world where day-to-day survival is the natural order (as it is in the animal kingdom), or in a relationship where one's being is sown into the very fabric of their environment (as with Eden), abstract thought is largely, if not wholly, irrelevant.

HUMANITY BECOMES FALLEN
BEFORE EVE EATS OF THE TREE

Again, it's worth noting that, as the story goes, Adam and Eve were in a perfect diametric relationship with the creation around them; they had no wants or fears or wills to be more than what they already were. And because of this harmony, abstract thought took a backseat to the existence found in the momentalism of their lives.[20] Again, Adam and Eve were in direct commune with God, the ultimate reality. And when reality is present — especially in the way it was described in The Garden — what is abstract is non-existent precisely because it is unneeded. That is to say that, when one is in possession of

---

[20] This may seem like a broad-sweeping claim until one considers that a function of abstract thought is often to imagine a scenario which does not exist in reality.

truth, that truth outshines abstract thought and relegates it to an untapped corner of consciousness.

But the serpent changes all of that. Again, even before the snake convinces Eve to eat the fruit of The Tree, it alters her forever by implanting into her mind an *idea*. And it is this idea that then forms numerous others, but none more dangerous than the one which manifests itself into doubt. (We might also just as easily say that the snake implants a doubt within her that manifests into an idea.) The serpent says to Eve that God is keeping something from her — something called power. And this power keeps Eve a mere servant of God, and this servitude keeps her from having an even better life than she currently enjoys. Poor Eve's newly formed brain must have been overflown with confusion. For, not only was one idea implanted within her, but several more ideas of even greater consequence were given to her immediately afterwards: servitude, power, a want to become more — all of these things were thrust upon Eve even before she bit into the fruit; but, with all of this in her mind, whatever she did from there would have been inconsequential. The seed had been planted: humanity was second rate; and not only that, but there was also more to the existence of life within The Garden, and it was God who kept them from it. Although the story does not say it directly, if Eve had even so much of a question as to whether any of what the serpent said was true, it was from that point that humanity became fallen. Her actual eating of the fruit was merely a symbolic gesture that consecrated the only forbidden act in all of Eden.

All too cleverly, the serpent created a weakness in humanity that was previously its strength: it played on humanity's relationship to reality by painting a picture of a world that was even greater than the one Adam and Eve were already experiencing. This is the first temptation: the desire to *become*. And through this newly forged desire to *be*, humanity drives a wedge between itself and its relationship to all Being. For, Being simply *is*; but humanity must now *become*. The serpent's temptation is nothing short of brilliant: not only are doubt and desire created in Eve's mind, but in its quest to attain what it had naturally possessed before its encounter with the snake, humanity loses its essence. Again, before their fall, humanity's place was secure. But the serpent created the doubt that there was more to life than what God had already given them. In fact, the serpent says that if they eat of The Tree their eyes will open and they will become like God itself. And this desire — the want to be God — has plagued humanity more than any other in the time since.

THE SERPENT AS THE HERO?

There is, however, another vantagepoint of The Fall which casts an entirely different shade of light on one of humanity's original stories. In what is typically viewed as a Gnostic interpretation of The Garden of Eden, the calibers and motivations of the players are often inverted from the mainline narrative, with God as the antagonist and the serpent as the hero. In many such Gnostic traditions, the original Hebrew God, Yahweh, is even seen as a kind of demonic presence that attempts to breed humanity into its pseudo-unconscious, ever-obedient servants. With a quick survey of the acts committed in the name of various religious practices and beliefs, one can easily see why many Gnostics saw the influences of Yahweh and a host of other religious godheads as non-beneficial to humankind. Acts carried out in the name of religious conviction are, of course, born in one's consciousness, and such a consciousness needs the proper molding in order to carry out the act in the first place.

For Adam and Eve, however, there was no actual "molding", per se, that needed to be done; for the shaping of a consciousness is only needed when that consciousness is capable of abstract thought — something that Adam and Eve appeared not to possess until the serpent implanted the idea into Eve's mind. (Again, humanity's fall takes place before the actual act of eating from The Tree is committed: once Eve has the notion in her mind that there was a greater existence beyond the one they currently enjoyed, the so-called "original sin" had occurred.) Yet, Adam and Eve were totally unaware of the concepts and ideas that would enable them to use the powers of their minds to a fuller extent. For, while it is true that the idea itself causes a great deal of humanity's difficulties, the ability to use the conceptual mind effectively is nevertheless key in unlocking the vast powers of human consciousness.

Of course, the debate we have raised here toys with the very issue of whether the ability to think abstractly is a gift or a curse. After all, nearly all human suffering can be traced back towards conceptualized thought, and yet, at the same time, to live without the ability for abstract thinking would mean that certain potentials of our individualized consciousnesses would go untapped. And regardless of the reader's own views on the biblical accuracies, an event like the one described at The Tree of Knowledge of Good and Evil is likely the moment in the development of human consciousness that we can trace our war's origins to. At the same time, however, the debate of abstract thinking's status is not one we seek to enter in to; the values of such things are best left to the conceptualized mind to tussle with. Our objective is to acknowledge that conceptualization is its own reality, and deal with it as such.

However, according to the biblical text and other human origin stories, the enormous potential for abstracted thought was not unveiled by God to original humanity — which begs the question: why? In early biblical text, Yahweh is often portrayed as a jealous, spiteful, wrathful, and generally uneasy being that seeks to gain dominance over opposing spiritual forces and other gods. Although it is unclear as to whether these other counteractive spiritual forces and various gods existed at the time, the behaviors and motivations of the god of The Garden of Eden story could be viewed, at the very least, as a precursor to such traits. Many in the Gnostic traditions readily support this line of thinking and accuse the motives of Eden's god as akin to those that the modern era traditionally aligns with a form of malevolence usually reserved for the likes of Satan. As mentioned previously, however, in various Gnostic perspectives it is the serpent who is viewed as humanity's champion. After all, God's strict orders attempt to keep Adam and Eve from the full tilt of knowledge, while it is the serpent that grants humanity the access to its conscious potential.

And though one could argue that while conceptualization has been the prime catalyst for human suffering and confusion, it could just as easily be said to be our greatest ability. After all, it is easy to see that so much of humanity's greatness can be attributed to the mesmerizing abilities afforded to us by the capacities of our consciousness. So, why would any being

— good or evil[21] — wish to hold humanity at bay from the vast and wonderful potentials that lie in wait through the abilities inherent within abstract thinking? Of course, positing the question in such a way makes it sound as though we are aware of God's intentions all along, and that it never planned on allowing humanity to eat of The Tree. On the other hand, one might relinquish the fact that is it completely possible that God had, in fact, planned to eventually allow for human beings to obtain the ability of thought we currently possess. Regardless, what is certain is that God had not wanted Adam and Eve to eat from The Tree at that time. And maybe time has everything to do with God's motivations.

For, as we have already stated in the early goings of our war — and as we will continue to do so consistently through it — conceptual knowledge and ideas in general can be extraordinarily dangerous; and yet, we have built the near entirety of our human consciousness around this structure. However, we must ask ourselves why, exactly, concepts and ideology have become so weaponized within our minds? The answer is quite possibly right there between the lines of that early biblical text: following the story as it's told, Adam and Eve had no knowledge of concepts, ideas, or few if any of the other general abilities our latter-day consciousnesses now enjoy. And being new beings themselves they would have had very little experience with things in general. Yet, in an instant their minds are transformed! They gain knowledge *about* things, and yet,

---

[21] The debate as to whether "God" (if such a thing exists) is "good" or "evil" is not one we are attempting to take on here. But most of humanity's classical notions of "God" are of a being that is wholly good, while the exact opposite is usually made of Satan.

they have no real knowledge *of* things. This is because they are afforded knowledge without the foundation of experience. And knowledge without experience is not really knowledge *of*: it is having an idea *about*. And such an idea can easily and most dangerously be mutated and mistaken for being real and true knowledge, or, even worse, reality itself. Adam and Eve went through no great trials. They had no adventure which taught them any lesson. They overcame no obstacle, faced no foe, endured no suffering, and, in the absence of those processes, learned no truths. All they came upon was the instantaneous downloading of some kind of "knowledge" into their minds which gave them shame and made them afraid.

And here is the difficulty not just for Adam and Eve, but for all human consciousness: knowledge *about* is not knowledge *of*, and yet the two are nearly always conflated. Knowledge *about* is second-handed: it comes to us from a source and is often given to that source by another source. Whereas knowledge *of* is verified by the self. Knowledge *of* is the experience and impactful impressions that come to compose what that self actually is, and that self is then able to give back to the experience and live within a double reflection of co-creativity. Knowledge *about* captures an individual and pins them into a conceptual corner which dictates the terms of existence to that consciousness or the person or thing that carries it. Knowledge *about* is incomplete at its very best, and wholly untrue and unreal at its worst. And not that knowledge *of* is knowledge in totality, but it does have its own kind of reality within itself precisely because there is no denying or debating it: it *is* what happened; it *is* the thing; it *is* that which is.

Adam and Eve had knowledge *about*, but what was terrifying for them was that they didn't even quite know about what. They had a vague interpretation of what things were — which is almost always the case with knowledge *about*. Original humanity's consciousness outgrew its holistic experience; and that is what caused its banishment from The Garden, and it is quite possibly what angered God. For, a being armed with thought must understand how to use it properly; otherwise such an armament is of the utmost danger to not only itself but the whole of creation, precisely because it can turn what is real into what is not through its misguided interpretations of phenomena. And if we take knowledge *about* — that is, conceptualization itself — as that which *is*, we then create false realities on top of false realities, eventually displacing reality itself.

And while the brand of consciousness humanity forged at The Tree is fraught with unlimited freedoms, one might argue that too much freedom without the proper guidance has led humanity down a dangerous path for many millennia. In fact, one could also argue that such freedom has been the bedrock of human being's existential dilemma: people are free, and yet we are enslaved by the utter weight of that freedom. There are no clear choices, no guideposts, no real knowledge *of* — only abstractions and vague interpretations *about*. But such abstractions are only mirages in the desert of life. Reality is our only salvation; yet we know not how to drink it in. Here is the danger. Here is the burden. Here is the crux and importance of our war.

THE SIGNIFICANCE OF EATING
OF THE TREE

Before we move further ahead, we must go back to some of the symbolism ensconced within the initial biblical story we've been exploring. Although we have pointed out that humanity became fallen even before the eating of the fruit, the act of ingesting something is nevertheless significant. Of course, as the story goes, after eating from The Tree, Adam and Eve were cast out of The Garden and forced to work the Earth by laboring through their every action — from childbirth to gathering food. But what was the fruit itself? Clearly, it was no ordinary food, but something that had drastic consequences — not all of which had to deal with Adam and Eve being banished from The Garden. So, we must ask ourselves: what was it that actually happened when the fruit was bitten into?

Taken metaphorically *or* evangelically, that the fruit was eaten holds vast significance. For, God's commandment was not that Adam and Eve should not look at The Tree, or smell it, or even touch it: it was that they were not to eat of it. After all (again, metaphorically or otherwise), what is seen or touched can be turned away from, just as what is heard or smelt will eventually peter out. But what is eaten becomes a part of the individual who ingests it. And not only does it become a part of that individual, but it gives that individual sustenance. Eating is a most intimate act that, on both physical and metaphorical levels, demonstrates our interconnectedness to the world around us. The process of eating is a truly odd magic: a living being takes something completely foreign to its body and uses it as fuel. Therefore, living beings are sustained by other organisms — many of which are or were at one time other living things — and the process of life's energy is simply transferred from one organism to the next in a never-ending symbiotic movement.

THE OPENING OF HUMANITY'S EYE

So, again, the act of eating is a significant one due to the fact that the eater and what is eaten merge and physically become one. However, there are certain kinds of foods that influence more than just the body alone; and it is this kind of paraphysical effect that was clearly felt once the fruit of The Tree of Knowledge was eaten from. For, as its namesake foretold, the real significance the ingestion of the fruit had on Adam and Eve was that it changed their *consciousness*. Most translations of the story say that the fruit of The Tree granted Adam and Eve sudden, previously unbeknown revelations; that is, the serpent was correct: once humanity became one with the fruit they did, in fact, have a different understanding of reality. Most famously, they realized they were naked and became ashamed, so they found clothing for themselves and hid from God. Because of a conscientious wedge driven into their minds — one that was clearly absent before eating from The Tree — Adam and Eve saw themselves as separate from nature; so, they felt the need to clothe their original bodies and, what's more, became ashamed of them. Instantaneously, they obtained an *idea* about who and what they were and, even worse, what they were *supposed* to be. Though, all the while their original beings were not only their actual natural states, but quite possibly also their strongest positions — as in those natural states they were in perfect harmony with both God and the manifested world of Being. Yet, they sought to change that originality because of their newly-found inclination towards shame — an inclination which was born from an idea. Following a want to become like God itself, this is the second act in mankind's eternally 'fruitless' quest to *become*.

REALITY CANNOT BE ACCESSED THROUGH THINKING ALONE

While realizing that it was the consciousness of humanity that was altered in disobeying God's only law is significant for our purposes, it then leads us to another direct question well worth asking: what was the fruit itself? Again, whether or not one believes the story to have taken place in actual history, clearly, the fruit was not merely just a fruit itself, but, so far as Adam and Eve were concerned, it may as well have been poison. And poison is not far off from this fruit's described nature. However, this biblical fruit was poison in a different form, for it did not so much tamper with the body but did something far more impactful to their overall beings: it diluted Adam and Eve's very minds. But what has the power to so heavily influence a mind that was formerly in such a close relationship with all of Being that it was able to commune directly with God itself? Clearly, if The Fall took place in history, the fruit acted only as the delivery system for something far greater. And if the events in The Garden were metaphorical, they point to something well beyond the mere act of the first sin. For, even though sin played an enormous role in The Fall's occurrence, it was not so much the sin itself that was significant; after all, sins can be forgiven. What is all the more dangerous, however, is that the pathway *to* sin was created once Eve contemplated ingesting the fruit of The Tree; and both the *idea of* and the *acting upon the idea* itself have been plaguing humanity ever since. More dangerous still is that the pathway opened up by Eve's mere contemplation is so commonly utilized that we cannot imagine ourselves as human beings without it. In fact, we have built up our entire beings around the process started by the serpent's influence on humanity's original consciousness.

For, the fruit was the process of thought itself. *The fruit was thinking.* Or, if taken literally, the eating of the fruit opened the eyes of humanity and created for us a complicated and arguably unnecessary consciousness. Because, again, as soon as humanity ate of The Tree, their minds saw division and separation where previously we knew only harmony. But had mankind's relationship to Eden or God changed? No — the relation itself remained as it was; only the consciousness about that relationship was altered; and it was a consciousness that drew dividing lines between all of Being, starting and ending with the self. And through these newly-minted conscious powers gained by an egocentric subjectivity, the thinking self immediately made distinguishments about its relation to all other Being, and thus lost the inherent powers of pure observation that come naturally to so many other kinds of consciousness we are aware of: animals, plants, and other varieties of living organisms all have perfectly conscientious relationships with their environment without the added need for abstract and dualistic thinking. But the kind of self-awareness gained from The Tree of Knowledge brought about a mode of thinking which separated the thinker from the object of the thought. As stated previously: the thinker both houses the thought and becomes influenced by it, and at the same time creates something which has its own life outside of the thinker. This is abstract thinking: it is an idea *of* or *about*. And in thinking of or about something — even though we are often trying to discover the truth of a thing — we are surreptitiously separating ourselves from what it is that is being thought about.

This is the danger of abstract thought: the thinker takes thought to be the reality when the thought has only glimpsed a small portion of reality, or, even worse, the thought is in no way aligned with reality whatsoever. Thoughts are only themselves, and yet our modernized human consciousnesses treat them as though they are realities which maintain an existence apart from those consciousnesses which house them. And so, thought creates its own para-reality next to reality itself. However, when thought deviates too far off course it becomes its own warped reality which immediately becomes detrimental not only to the thinker and all those who subscribe to the thought itself, but such off-track thoughts can have vast and devastating consequences on the legitimate being of true and actual reality. And yet, it is this kind of "thinking" that we as modern-day human beings have built our entire beings and society on and around. We, in this war, will refer to the conscious process of modern thought which takes place within the human mind as "*conceptualization*". And we seek to expose and elaborate upon the notion that concepts themselves were the initial cause of the fall of humanity, just as they will continue to be so until we eliminate them altogether and replace them with a new modality of being. For, as the story of Eden reveals to us, reality is lost through the process of conceptualized thought. That is, one cannot truly comprehend what reality is through the process of thinking as our minds have come to implement it.

THE THOUGHT IS NOT THE THING: REALITY CANNOT EXIST WHERE ONE INTERJECTS THOUGHTS INTO BEING

As we have already discussed, even though conceptualization often drives a wedge between the thinker and the reality, nevertheless, thoughts are, in fact, often attempts to unite the thinker with reality. A great many thoughts take place in order to attempt to solve a problem or insert oneself into a situation. For, again, thought is often an effort to gain knowledge *of.* However, when one is perfectly aligned with reality there is nothing to gain. After all, if reality is achieved then all is already known, or, more likely, there is nothing to know given that the being and the reality are simply working together symbiotically. So, we must understand very clearly that ideas separate the thinker from both the thought and all other Being itself, and thrusts the thinker into an abstracted, metaphysical realm of his own mental constructions.

Thoughts are not the things themselves: if one were to think of a rock, the thought *about* the rock is not the actual rock itself, and yet, we often treat it as though it were: we respond to our thoughts as if they contained physical matter — often times inflicting bodily pain on ourselves and others through the mere product of our thoughts alone.[22] And it was this idea *about* a thing or state that ultimately banished humanity from a kind of paradise-relationship it likely enjoyed with all other Being (which was precisely what the story of Eden attempts to convey). Humanity had an idea *of* reality that was not in line

---

[22] We will delve into this more in the chapter on "Language" in Part II.

with how the being of reality *actually* operated. And if we look at God as the ultimate reality itself, we can see that although it was in fact "God" who ostracizes Adam and Eve from Eden, it was really the gulf created by Adam and Eve's concepts *about* reality that led them beyond Eden's gates. God, as a presence, was simply no longer there; *how could it have been?* As a reality that exists totally and completely *with*, God could not openly exist alongside a consciousness that went about the business of abstracting itself from reality (that is, God) through its own consciousness. In the parameters set up within Eden, to be with God was to be with reality. So, how could God have been present when humanity chose to experience the world through a consciousness that filtered everything through itself via an abstraction? God was the reality, and Eden was its earthly playground. But mankind chose to exit it through the process of its own cognition. Humanity's thoughts *of* and *about* are not God's meditative being *for* and *wit*

THE WEB OF CONCEPTION

Humanity's harmonious existence *with* came to an end because of the ideas that were constructed about both metaphysical and physical Being. Such constructs then produced a particular consciousness which further produced a very specific relationship to phenomena itself. Again, this was a construction born of mere ideas, yet those ideas separated humanity from the natural connection we enjoyed prior to our ingestion of concepts. It appears as though concepts were too much for human consciousness to handle initially, and things have not gotten much better in the time since. In fact, being that our minds have done nothing but gather more and more concepts, one might argue that things for us — both physically and psychologically — have only gotten worse. For, in order to mentally interact with and sustain a singular concept, many other concepts must be born or sustained. It is the same thing with any web of lies: other lies must be told to prop up the initial fib. Or, even more simply stated: thoughts must beget other thoughts. This *is* the process of thought: one thought leads to others which leads further still to others. However, if the initial thought is immediately out of step with reality (as all thoughts *must* by their very definition be), then how can thinking solve the problem of its original purpose, which, of course, is to attain reality? The irony is thick. However, that's not to say that thought cannot attain reality when a consciousness is cleared away of all conceptualization. Yet, in a kind of pure consciousness completely free from the abstractions given to the mind under conceptualization, the process of thought would look so different that it would hardly seem like thinking in the way we currently understand and experience it.

EDEN'S SPIRITUAL SIGNIFICANCE AS A METAPHOR

It is not our intent to make a claim one way or another about the historicity of the event, however, regardless of one's beliefs, the metaphor of Eden must be further explored. Though, if we were to look at Eden not so much as a place but more so as a state of harmonious being, what happens to both our understanding of the story and our past and current human condition? After all, regardless of Eden's material existence, across all religions the physical being of a thing is understood as a mere a gateway to a spiritual awakening. And even if Eden did have an actual physical existence, looking at it from the religious point of view, it only existed as a stage for Adam and Eve's spiritual life — as any religious apologist would argue of any happening or circumstance. Therefore, regardless of what one believes about its physical existence, Eden's spiritual significance must be carefully examined.

Going further, one can only attain a spirituality through a certain kind of consciousness; so, it is that consciousness we hope to solicit through our examination of Eden as a spiritual metaphor. To that end, it may best serve us to see Eden as a kind of original conscious state of being. After all, one can physically be in paradise, but if one's focus is elsewhere it is difficult to enjoy or appreciate it. Similarly, one could be in any kind of imaginable hell, and if the right frame of mind were achieved the physical environment or circumstance would be inconsequential. So, as with all things, it is the state of the consciousness that is important. And one can dictate one's own state by determining one's conscientious position. Spiritually and metaphorically, Eden's aftermath could be understood as something which continues to happen to us at every waking moment. Taken as two beings who existed in reality, we are generations upon generations removed from Adam and Eve's existence. But taken as a metaphor, Eden is still alive and unfolding within us; and being so, we have a vast amount of power to be able to actively manipulate the consciousness common to all of humanity; and, what's more, that common consciousness, in turn, produces the very lives we lead.

The Garden of Eden was a state of being whether or not one believes in its actually having existed: in physical existence or metaphorical lore, the effect and result come out to equal the same thing. *How* the events of The Garden took place is practically immaterial: it is the result that we aim to deal with. The same rule applies to Adam and Eve: it matters not whether they were two actual human beings or Adam was a metaphor for humankind and Eve represented its general subconsciousness; what exists within the minds of humanity today is the product of either the actual historical event or the allegorical fable, but either way the result and must be dealt with properly.

COMPOUNDED CONCEPTION

The state of our consciousness is the only relevant thing. Everything we as human beings do and experience — from physical action to metaphysical thought — is born of and dies within consciousness; without it we are mere physical shells. It is our consciousness that shapes our comprehension of the world around us, and this comprehension *of* determines our relationship *with* that world. And yet, our consciousness *of* any given thing is something gifted to us through antiquity: what is known and experienced is conscientiously passed on from one generation to the next. That is, through each generation — both biologically and conceptually — we pass on the operationality of our brains and the minds they contain therein.

Biologically, our brain's physical structure and capacities are cultivated through its workings with phenomena and its evolution through time. On the conceptual end, the transfer of concepts unfolds right before our eyes when we realize how we teach our children about the world. After all, infants are not born with beliefs: beliefs are given to the child by a parent who is likewise informed by any number of beliefs garnered through experience or abstracted thought. Even the child's own name is not really its own, for it is no more a Samuel than it is a Maria or a Stephen. The name is a placement bestowed upon the child, and the child then takes it as its own. It is the same with any label, abstract concept, or belief.

A similar image of infantile humanity can be painted: our ancestors lacked the complicated cognitive structures put together by eons of conceptual thought. In humankind's earliest days there were no countries or nationalities or political relations. The original human mind had not developed the concept of preeminence: it simply existed alongside and *with* the world; only when it abstracted itself from that existence *with* did there spring up a necessity for the kinds of dualistic relations that have become so commonplace today. So, metaphorically or not, whatever it was that happened after Adam and Eve ate from The Tree of Knowledge, that happening was passed on through Consciousness from one generation to the next. And very quickly the human mind began to develop. And with that development came the existence of knowledge. And the knowledge obtained about ourselves and the world was and still is constantly being informed by the previous knowledge we've obtained. So, knowledge is a complicated building process which only begets more and more of itself.

However, something very-very dangerous can happen in the acquisition of this knowledge: it can be incomplete or misinformed. Often the means by which knowledge is obtained is unrefined, and this unrefinement leads to only partial comprehension about a given thing. The danger, however, is that the knowledge garnered through a raw and incapable consciousness is almost always taken to be true, and then that so-called truth is acted on, yielding disastrous results. Therefore, our process of discernment and knowledge-building needs constant refining. Unfortunately, however, conceptualization will not let this refinement take place in the ways in which it needs to in order to delineate full-fledged fact from a partial truth or an all-out fiction; the mind's listlessness is mainly due to the attachments it harbors in perceiving the world, and these attachments impede the mind from seeing beyond its own preconditioning. Of course, given that the conceptual mind has structured itself to acquire more and more knowledge *of* and *about*, these attachments have become natural. Unfortunately, however, in an ever-dynamic universe, acquisition is only useful for so long. Adaptation is a consummately better bedfellow, which is why evolution is key for any survival — biologically or conscientiously.

The consciousness humanity has set up for itself is based on identifying various modes of information and utilizing that information after its having been processed. Of course, those various bits of information are also informed by whatever it is our minds have processed previously. A large blue square is only such because our minds have drawn distinctions about size, color, and shape, and those distinctions have come to inform other kinds of information which in turn will serve to inform others without end. As conceptual beings, the predispositions of our consciousness in some way hamper our capacity to simply be *with* a thing though complete and total observation.

This is the beauty of science: science is a surrendering of ego and belief to a series of observations. Of course, science is not impervious to the kinds of pitfalls a singular mind might also fall victim to, but science is at least more likely to stave off belief in favor of pure observation. However, being that science is merely the observation of repetition, there are certain patterns that are constantly being missed due to the fact that one's capacities for observation are limited.

So, in a consciousness set up by beliefs about the information it has gathered through its limited observations of phenomena, we can easily see where our alignment with reality might not be ironclad. The modern human mind is also constantly interpreting its experiences, which only causes both it and those experiences to further drift out into the nether regions of abstraction. And these abstracted interpretations then inform our situationality — and vice versa — until we find ourselves in an entangled web of skimpy observations and half-baked philosophical and existential notions — all of which we amalgamate and take to be reality.

Let us also not forget that a great many of these beliefs and notions about the ways in which things (including our own selves) are impressed upon us by culture, religion, political intentions, and an educational system that has propagated the bewildered patterns of the modern mind. The conceptual mind is so intent on knowledge acquisition that it takes in information without processing it through the best filter it has: its own natural, unhampered state — which, because of this desire to devour any information it can, have atrophied. In the modern era, most people have accepted a narrative about their own relation to the world which has been given to them from other concepts. Very few have pioneered their own philosophical existence and stood up to the various conscientious oppressions one encounters on a daily basis. Our minds take what they've been given so that we can make the most sense of our own lives and our relation to Being at large .... It is not difficult to see why confusion looms like a dragon above the world.

AN EDEN WITHIN US

So, concepts are delivered through the vehicles of systems like culture, religion, politics, science, broad-sweeping beliefs, and others — all of which can be useful and beautiful in their own rights. However, in order to attain that which actually *is* — in order to be wholly *with* — all of those things must be set aside so that we might regain that direct conversation and connection with what has previously been referred to as "God", but might simply be better understood as reality itself.

For, after having eaten from The Tree (whatever it may or may not have been), the consciousness of humanity shifted: human beings became more aware *of* things, but at the same time, became more detached *from* them. We experienced a great abstraction of our own selves from the Being around us. The even harmony humanity enjoyed within Eden was nowhere to be found outside of its gates. Although, outside of the gates all is not lost.

Viewed as a spiritual state, The Garden is really something hopeful because it means that it can be re-entered. Viewed in this capacity, Eden is not some faraway place, but an unexplored realm within our conscientious reach. And that is what this war is about: it is about going back into that inner garden and reconnecting with ourselves and reality. Because Eden is akin to a beautiful prison, and, having been cast out one could argue that it has been a blessing that we must now find our way back to it. However, in this journey we must work to regain what has been lost; but as it is with all good lessons and circumstances, the degree of meaning one gets out of the journey is equivalent to the work put in and realization of its significance.

Truly, whether or not it once existed on a historical timeline, The Garden today is in our own minds; it is a relationality between ourselves and the god spoken of in ancient allegories. And within our own originality as human beings we have an innate and forceful power waiting to be tapped. For, within all of us lies that original being which communed so effortlessly with the reality it encountered within Eden. And it is really that originality which serves to drive and empower us. Outside of The Garden we have come to acquire knowledge through the form of conception and a cerebral comprehension *of*. However, this mental construction is not so much an evil in itself, but it has colored our minds, leading them to prejudice, desire, and a want to be become something other than what we already are; and these desires have ultimately brought us away from ourselves and away from our original being.

But this war is about reconnecting. Eden is within. It is the process — the way we have attained and manufactured the knowledge — which has both extracted us and kept us from its gates.

When humanity swallowed the fruit of conception it took itself out of the present and set its sights on something beyond what presently existed. Yet, in that search we have not only lost the present, but we have also lost the desire to discover our own original selves in favor of an attempt to become something more. In Eden humanity was originally tempted by the power of knowledge, but that temptation is now more alluring than ever. And, again, it is not that knowledge is evil or something that should not be pursued, but more so that the way we have set up our minds to intake knowledge has been blackened by the concepts which have come to structure it. Only the pure mind can truly attain reality; and knowledge has nothing at all to do with one's relationship to what *is*. But in our conceptual minds, to be powerful is akin to godliness itself, and we all seek out our own perch on the hierarchy of power. Ironically, however, the kind of information we attain through knowledge *of* is the opposite of godliness: both the process and acquisition of abstracted, conceptual knowledge drive us away from what *is* — which can only be truly comprehended through an immersive, coexistent being *with*. And in another heavy irony, because of our desire to attain power, we are now in an unending struggle for it — nearly all of which further keeps us from having any, or, if we do, we must then continually battle to maintain it.

Whereas all being was without power relations inside The Garden, outside of it we are forced to create our own balance. Eating from the tree of conceptualization meant that we gained ideas *of*, yet those ideas are not the reality we enjoyed before having fragmented our minds. And that is what our fallen state is: it is a place that makes our all-too-human selves what we are; and what we are as human beings carries with it its own kind of fierce beauty; but we take our fierceness too far and disregard our beauty too often. Our values have become skewed through a lack of our capacity to accept things as they are — including our own selves. After all, when acceptance is present there is no room for anything to the contrary. Acceptance is the key. In it, our subtle, yet true powers quietly erupt. For acceptance is the antidote for our aspirations towards godliness. When acceptance is the dominant mode it squeezes out all want and desire; and in this state our motivation is based solely on attaining what is, and one becomes wholly incorruptible. But through want and desire to become, all the sins — classical or otherwise — are put into play. So, we can clearly see that the keys to salvation are forged not by some outer locksmith, but by our own internal craftsmanship.

Through Eden's exodus our humanity has chosen the path of becoming and want, which has led us to disharmony and disconnection. After all, we must ask ourselves: why would God not have wanted us to have eaten from The Tree? Clearly it was not because, as the serpent promised, we would then become rivals of God — for our newfangled conscientious state not brought us further from God's presence, but further from our own originally powerful state. What makes entirely more sense is that God wished to keep us in a state of being *with* so that we might continually enjoy its creation to our utmost capacity and continue in our direct and reciprocating relationship with reality (that is, with God). One's motivation is always and forever the telltale.

And yet, there is a certain beauty about our fallen state. For, in spite of this disharmony we remain redeemable. And although we may not be in direct connection *with* it, we still exist *alongside* that ever-attainable reality which consummately waits for our reciprocity. But until we accept simple being, we will always be in the race of complicated becoming.

Our war is a battle back to Eden. And we are presently as far from that sacred garden as could be, and we can trace our disconnect back to a want to become and an insatiable thirst for power and knowledge — the desire to be God itself. Although, it is not our objective to condemn, criminalize, or label these common human traits as good or bad; doing so is a task for the value judgements of language games we must refuse to play. Our job throughout this war will be to observe and report, and through our thorough exposing of the unfettered ways in which things are, we will begin to strip humanity's pervasive consciousness of the conceptions it holds about the world. However, the choice will be ours. And hopefully we will leave behind judgements in favor of acceptance. Hopefully we turn our focus towards where and what we are, not where and what we wish to be. Hopefully we will come to understand that this war is waged within our consciousness at virtually every waking moment. Hopefully we will come to discover that Eden is not only within us, but that it is the very earth we walk. Ironically enough, as we go along in our war, we may even come to realize that we were not so much thrown out of The Garden as did we choose to leave it by molding our conceptualized consciousness in such a way that Eden no longer became recognizable.

But Eden is here before us. Though, it is our choice whether we wish to re-enter it or stay eternally locked outside its gates, only occasionally even thinking to peer in.

THE FOREST OF CONCEPTION

The entirety of this war — or any other — is about conception. And although we have already identified and touched on it previously, being that it is *the* enemy we are fighting in our philosophical war, we need to fully work through what conceptualization is before we can combat it with maximum effectiveness.

A concept is a thought or idea that has no actual existence outside of our own minds. It is a live notion playing out within a consciousness or group of consciousnesses. The interaction of various concepts and the utilization and integration of those thoughts to build still more ideas or implement those thoughts into Being and phenomena is conceptualization. In the way in which we have come to structure our modern consciousness, conception has become the general modality of thinking itself; it is the vehicle or the environment that enables and sustains cognition, impressions, beliefs, notions, images, perceptions, theories and theorems, hypotheses, views, assumptions and suppositions, codes, postulations, abstractions, descriptions, principles, speculations, interpretations, operations, axioms, visions, doctrines, creeds, governances, dogmas, canons, tenets, estimations, judgments, philosophies, and others; all of these and more are various houses marching under the banner of conceptualization; in their particularized states they are specific conceptual forms — each with certain functions — like various parts of a machine working together to establish an operation. Therefore, when the term "conceptualization" is used in our war it is meant to allude to this family of words and their extenuating utilities. If the aforementioned list of words are the parts, "conceptualization" refers to the whole as a unified scheme — the overarching category which hosts the subjective, individualized particulars.

And it is extremely important that this scheme and its individualized houses be elucidated. For — ironically enough, *through* the use of concepts — the human consciousness has become so extraordinarily powerful that it has come to endow itself with a capacity to actually go so far as to create a reality (or host of realities) that previously had no existence. Put another way, these realities are almost always birthed through conceptualization and only then become "real" when reinforced by other concepts — which, of course, begs the question as to whether or not they can actually be labeled as "real" or a "reality" in the first place. Though, this sparks a further and entirely relevant debate about what "reality" actually is — which, epistemologically speaking, is a quarrel that has raged through various philosophical and theological sects and institutions for several millennia with no clear end in sight.

But what we need to understand is that our war is an attempt to recapture true and objective reality. Because, based upon our monumental over-reliance on conceptualization, our human consciousness has created a phenomenology that it believes to be in step with actuality, when, in truth, what we are experiencing is nothing more than an infinite amount of singular concepts all helixed together to form a grand construction that we have come to live out and accept as "reality". When, in *actual* reality, this faux-phenomenological construct is its own quagmire that we have simply taken for granted by assuming that our way of perception is somehow automatically aligned with reality as it is. Because we have grown up in the forest of conceptualization, we cannot see its many trees. So, not only are we, in our war, asserting the actuality of a tangible and objective reality, but we are further stating here that we cannot access such a reality through the consciousness we have set up for ourselves.[23]

Again, it is extraordinarily naive to assume that a consciousness constructed of and executed through conceptualization is capable of detecting what is real and what is not. Moreover, there is great danger in assumptions in general due to the fact that the human consciousness is powerful enough to take what was conceptual at its onset and morph it into a reality based on its own misguided perceptions. That is to say that one of humanity's many gifts is that we have been bestowed with the powers of reality-creationism ourselves: we can make what *is* disappear just as easily as we give what *is not* an eternal life. More so, almost anything created by the human consciousness can have a life both inside and outside of the creator; this means that a human consciousness can take something internal and externalize it, which gives the thing a life in both subjectivity and objectivity. And in this, too, a tremendous power is granted to both the creator and the

---

[23] A great deal more will be said about this in the chapter on "Vim, Verity, and Consciousness".

creation: thoughts, opinions, or observations that one thinker externalizes can become internalized by another thinker's subjectivity; when this happens, a reality is thus generated *in objectivity* through the very act of one thinker having influenced another's subjective state.

The entirety of human existence is an example of this phenomenon, but it is possibly most easily demonstrated in art: a work of art is initially an internally an undefined notion or feeling that comes forth and is expressed in some kind of form to the external world. Conceptualization, of course, has a similar process: actions often originate from an individual's consciousness — whatever form that consciousness might hold; it is important to understand the power in this clearly, because, as human beings, we are endowed with the very tumultuous ability to create and even manipulate the external world just from our subjective thoughts. In a very real way, our thoughts are a most potent kind of physical matter in and of themselves.

For, as our war rages on we hope to expose the way in which these various forms of conceptualization all support and sustain one another in one large illusory fashion. And, as in any flimsy system, once a single component is yanked from any part of the structure, the entire thing crumbles like a house of cards. However, it should be made clear that we are not suggesting that thought itself should be discarded as a tool, but more so that we must recognize that the methodology by which we implement our mental capacities has been corrupted through thinking's broad-sweeping use of concepts — all of which distance the thinker from the object of her thought through abstraction.

CONCEPTUAL EVOLUTION

But conceptualization is a relationship, namely, between human consciousness and either itself or external phenomena. That is, conception has become a product of humanity's conscious interaction with both its interior self and with the physical environment that individual consciousness reacts to. Most dangerously, it has become the vehicle by which the human mind has come to do the business of comprehending its own conscious being. Therefore, all conceptualization is an internalization — an inward turning toward the self, which then processes, regurgitates, and externalizes that turning into some sort of material or metaphysical manifestation. Conceptualization is subjective interpretation; and when a subjective interpretation becomes ratified in the majority of other minds, that interpretation then becomes a way of processing which is then passed on virally from consciousness to consciousness, eventually altering the actual physical structure of the brain. Miraculously, mass conceptualization is evolution on a metaphysical level which then becomes physical: when a concept is born and utilized by enough minds, a new mode of being is created (whether metaphysical or physical), and this mode will have an immediate impact on the actual physical structure of the brain itself. New modes of physical being will affect the mental approach of an organism just as new cognitive approaches will alter the physical nature of the organism.

And such evolutionary changes (whether they be physical or cognitive) often begin with a single individual who can pass on the trait. Yet, on the contentious level, these influential concepts-turned-modes are initially the collective agreements of only a few subjective, and, hence, limited viewpoints. However, if these modes of conscious operations come to be accepted by the majority, the once subjective operations are then falsely viewed as objective truths even though they were once merely ways of thinking which were born and sustained by subjectivity and, being so, will always remain at a distance from objective reality.

And these once subjective-mental-constructions-turned-mainstream-thought-patterns serve as a kind of blueprint by which other subsequent minds can follow. However, the general problem is that these blueprints which are born and carried out by subjective minds are taken as objective fact by the subsequent minds adopting their ideas or patterns, and this blind adherence to previous concepts nullifies any possibility of a unique approach by other subjective minds; that is, because a mind has already inherited patterns from an ancestry, its own unique subjectivity is subverted or brushed aside. And the minds adopting the ancestral cognition treat these given patterns like laws when, in fact, laws are themselves the reifications of a kind of conceptualization.

THERE ARE NO LAWS, ONLY RELATIONS

After all, laws are principles implemented to uphold order in either the phenomenological or metaphysical realms, and are always general abstractions that exist only so long as the framework which instantiated and installed them is upheld. Governances, operations, systems, no matter how concrete they seem, are — when emanating from a human level — put together by subjective and limited beings, and are thus in and of themselves subjective and limited. Yet, even what we think of as universal, cosmic, or natural laws are not so. In actuality there are no laws — only relations which are contingent on subjective interactions.[24] We can only know and describe the relationship between the subject and the object — or the self and the thing — and that relationship is always temporal because of the continually fluctuating understanding of either our self or the thing in question or observation. What we think of as a "law" is only the repetition of a pattern, but all patterns are subject to change when they interact with other forces or circumstances, or the capacity of the observer is altered. Furthermore, it is our conceptual mind which labels something as a law or pattern in the first place, but our powers of observation are limited by what "laws" we have come to recognize. Of course, these "laws" are propped up on the unstable foundations of our limited capacities for comprehending them, and once those capacities are altered by a new force, pattern, or observation, the "law" changes. So, again, a "law" is just an observation we come to recognize because of the relationship our constructed minds have with phenomena, and most of these capacities for thought and observation have been given to us through antiquity by the recognition of other "laws" and patterns that may very well no longer be accurate, yet we take them to be the cornerstones

---

[24] Even scientific laws are completely dependent on subjective agreement: scientifically speaking, there are no laws, only forces which act in similar ways on a given (set of) subject(s).

of reality.......Unfortunately, though, the true nature of laws is almost always disregarded.

OUR COMPREHENSION OF REALITY IS FILTERED THROUGH CONCEPTS

However incomplete, we often turn the interaction between self and that which we perceive as other than the self into something which we can utilize and relate to; this effort is an attempt to fill in the gaps of our limited understanding of phenomena. Such interactions — which themselves are merely relationships — are turned into laws and systems or methods and structures which become the foundations of our human comprehension of the world. But the world as we experience it is not necessarily the world as it actually *is*, but only as it appears in relation *to* us; and that relation is given to us through an ancestry of consciousness that was formulated in a very particular way by the concepts which have come to dominate our thought process.

The concepts we formulate are merely functional: they are tools we use to better and more accurately comprehend Being itself. Moreover, they act as rules of engagement when encountering nearly anything at all and the parameters set up by the framework of conceptualization give us a series of guideposts by which to navigate through nature and its ever-flourishing human byproducts. Often, we see that very stringent criterion has been placed around these conceptualizations: there are always rules as to how things operate in the universe, and humanity has done its very best to attempt to capture and comprehend those happenings. But there soon arises a problem when attempting to rein-in even the most simplistic natural laws: such "laws" must always be modified. This is because conceptualization is simply not tidy. And being that concepts are continually utilized to process reality, our understanding of reality is always filtered through the concepts we utilize to comprehend that reality; therefore, in a conscientious catch twenty-two, the concept attempts to base itself on the reality it perceives, yet the reality is only able to be ascertained through the concept. It is like having an understanding about a mountain by traveling a particular trail: while the hiker might achieve certain realities and encounter various points on the mountain because of the trail's path, she will never understand the entirety of the mountain itself given that she only uses a singular roadway to interact with it. And yet, it is that roadway that, at the same time, has allowed her to climb the mountain in the first place.

THE CONCEPTUAL CONSCIOUSNESS'S DISTANT RELATIONSHIP WITH REALITY

What's more is that in a consciousness controlled by conceptualization, the very act of seeking is something of a departure from reality. For, whatever it is that is experienced via the prism of conception is done so through a very particular process which is limited by the capacities of the concepts employed in the search. However, unlike with conception, reality — or, that which *is* — does not need to be sought out in order to have an effect on the seeker; for, being what *is*, reality already exists and is readily present and accessible: reality needs only to be recognized and, through that recognition, mindfully experienced. Usually, however, the experience itself is hampered by the concepts attached to the consciousness which does the experiencing.

Conception seeks. It must seek because it is not with truth; therefore, it must reach out beyond itself in an attempt to gain truth. In fact, to seek is the mission and the fuel of conception. Of course, if truth was already present and recognized as such, the search would be unnecessary. Yet, in conceptualization, the search is never-ending precisely because by implementing concepts the truth can never be attained. To understand, to grasp, or to gain are just a few of conception's main attempts. But every attempt is a failure as soon as it is implemented. Because the thought, idea, or concept, is not the thing itself; it is not reality, but only a singular consciousness's attempt at a relationship *with* reality. And yet we have built an entire civilization on the bedrocks of thought; and therein lies the problem: how does one revolt against the foundation? How can we reduce the pillars to rubble without doing the same to the structure (presuming we'd like to keep it intact)?

It should be stated again here that it is not the intention of this philosophical counterassault to strike down thinking itself, so to speak. But we are in full-scale revolt against the way in which thinking, as a total process, has been reared, glorified, and thus implemented — or, more accurately, imposed. Here we encounter a very valuable, yet simplistic question which both exposes the fallacy that thought is a necessary utility when attempting to harness the core of reality, and at the same time accurately summarizes the base cause for our war: *if thinking is supposed to gain us access to reality, then why do we need it in the first place?* Reality, by its very ontology, should be ultimately and inexhaustibly accessible. And yet, we are continually attempting to gain access to truth through cognition. We seem to be forever at a distance from that which we wish to acquire — unable to comprehend or understand why a thing is a certain way. From scientists and engineers to philosophers and athletes and nearly every pursuit or occupation in between, in each human undertaking we appear to strive for something not yet attained. We are in constant *pursuit of* rather than *in harmony with*. And by engaging in that pursuit there is an unspoken recognition that we are somehow out of step with the actuality of things. Through these ceaseless pursuits we seem to be confessing our inability to access the underlying secrets of the general operationality of things — all of which are, for some reason, just beyond our reachings. That the universe and its renderings remain a grand mystery to us is the premise for almost all spiritual, philosophical, existential, and scientific inquiry.

But why is this mystery so shrouded to us? If reality is what *is*, and yet at the same time reality is also inaccessible to us, then, clearly, we are not directly engaged with reality; that is to say that if we need to use concepts to understand the way that things supposedly are, then we are removed by some degree from reality. Therefore, it is not that reality is a mystery to be solved, but, more accurately, *we* are a mystery to be solved. And the objective of this work is to uncover how we became that mystery, and ultimately to liberate us from it.

This can only be done, however, by delving further and more brutally into the nature of conceptualization itself. In war, often a target must be blitzed in order to break the front lines; in this war, conceptualization has such a grasp on our very way of being that we must constantly restate and expose its many infiltrations so as to begin to free ourselves from its grime. Again, because conceptualization is a falsehood it must be constantly altered, exhaustingly realigning itself like a lie that gets deeper and more intricate the more it's perpetuated. And that is precisely what concepts are: they are untruths (or, at the very least, half-baked notions *of* truth). Although they are not necessarily intentionally misleading, concepts must maintain a distance from reality in order to survive. For, ironically, although concepts are intended to be used as tools in order to obtain reality, if reality had already been attained, the concept would be useless. After all, once the house has been built the hammer is no longer necessary.

Almost uniformly, we think of scientific or philosophic observation as being objective and unbiased; this is true to the extent that those observations are unbiased in relation to a current mode of thought or a certain ability or way of seeing. However, what is more accurate is that observations are generated by certain capacities, theories, ideas, and patterns which came before them and vice versa: the observation is a product of our ability to observe, just as thoughts are a product of our ability to think; our ability to observe and to think are products of those tools we utilize for observation and thought that have been corrupted by the false-flag operations of conceptualization which champion the fabricated promises that the only way to truth is through their utilities. Again, it simply cannot be stated enough in these initial battles that concepts come from human beings who are themselves limited beings attempting to gain accessibility to an ultimacy they have separated themselves from through their very searching for it.

This war is an effort to reconnect us with our natural state of being. Ultimately, this is a war of consciousness and spirit. But our difficulty is that we must fight concepts with our own conceptualized minds. After all, we can only fight with the weapons we have at our disposal. However, with any luck, those weapons that currently battle against us will be the same ones that liberate us in the end.

Of course, if the consciousness of a being changes, everything within the scope of that consciousness has the capacity to change along with it. And this is a war to attain reality itself through a conscientious shift, which is why we have stated that this war —though pasted onto pages and not in fields of physical combat — is the most important war of all time. It is a struggle to regain our humanity — a humanity freed from the oppressions of thousands of years of occupation from conceptualized processes of thought. What's more is that this war is of the most massive scale possible, because it includes and affects every portion of consciousness for every human being in existence. In fact, every conscious movement made by human being contributes to this struggle either in support of it, or, often unwittingly, combating it. This happening is innocent enough: we, in our human experience, believe that we operate within reality as it is and as it always has been. And yet, our concepts *about* the world have given us an understanding *of* the world. We are our conceptions. And those conceptions are what we dub as reality. This notion is paradoxical due to the fact that conceptions remove us from what is real, yet, in the fabrication of our post-Eden humanity, conceptualization has been our mainstay, and hence, that which most deeply penetrates our consciousness — a consciousness that is the mediating tool between ourselves and reality. Therefore, our consciousness, cancered with the pox of conceptualization, has become an unreliable agent by which to decipher reality itself.

THE ISOLATION OF THE OBSERVER

Conceptions are ideas we have about anything at all, regardless of how aligned with truth that idea actually is. Again, what's important to acknowledge is that the thought is not the thing itself. The idea is merely a portrayal. The thinking that takes place within the individualized consciousness is purely an isolated event removed from the actuality of the object of the thought, or of that which the individual consciousness observes. The process of thought, as human beings have come to cultivate it, is a matter of separating one's self from the thing in which one observes or concentrates on. However, in truth, the observer and the observed are not actually separate happenings or beings. Misguidedly, we have come to see the event and the consciousness observing it as distinctive happenings because of the concepts we have developed about and within our own individualized consciousness and its relationship to what we have come to distinguish as Otherness. We believe to have a certain comprehension of an operation or entity because of our ability to accurately describe it or predict its actions; but the description of a process is not the process itself, no matter how seemingly accurate it is depicted. Furthermore, an individualized consciousness is only able to observe an operation or an entity through the faculties it possesses. And in a consciousness absorbed by conceptualization, the ability for observation will be forever tainted through the filters of the concepts which compose it.

In the way in which a marine biologist cannot know what it is to be a fish no matter how long he studies one, by implementing conceptualization alone, we cannot truly know what the reality of a given thing is, either phenomenologically or metaphysically. We can study that which appears, but we can never know it in its fullest sense, at least, not through the utilization of conceptualization. Concepts keep us from reality precisely because they are reconstructions *of* reality. And what's more: concepts keep us from ourselves by veiling us in the garbs of the now convoluted operations of our very own individual consciousness. And that's the enemy's trick: it pretends to be our ally by giving us an apparent way by which to comprehend the phenomena which encircles us. However, the means by which we must utilize conceptualization separates us from the thing itself; and we then come to know phenomena only as something to be studied or thought about, and not actually experienced as an intricate part of actuality. But it is in that unobstructed interaction *with* actuality that our being can be discovered. And in that discovery, we can bring forth a being which is well beyond that which we have labeled as merely "human".

CONCEPTION OF VS BEING WITH

The better our descriptions become, the more accurately we can predict a certain happening. But knowledge *of* a thing is not harmonious *being with* the actuality of the thing. And that existence *with* is the reality we seek. That is to say that "knowledge of" and "existence with" are two very different kinds of experiences. In fact, the *being with* is the experience itself, while *knowledge of* is always divisive — separating the thing from the observer. Knowledge of is not being with. Conception is knowledge of. Reality, truth, and actuality is being with.

Conceptions have existence only because a consciousness gives them one. And what an individual consciousness extracts from an observation is based solely on the resources it has at its disposal— resources given to it through the consciousnesses that have preceded it. That is to say that the individualized consciousness is inherited from the beings which have come before it. And an individual consciousness then, in turn, perpetuates those given resources because they are the only faculties it has at its disposal. This is precisely how conceptualization breeds: an experience or an idea is obtained about a thing, and the individual consciousness attaches itself to that idea or experience. And the idea or experience we garner is something that comes from beyond ourselves, yet, at the same time, we allow it to modify our consciousness. Of course, a consciousness becomes what it attaches itself to, and in doing so it creates notions about what it is and how it operates. Such self-fabricated notions control the existentialism of a given consciousness. And yet, in actuality — *precisely because the ideas it possesses are not real* — the conceptualized consciousness is simultaneously removed from the conceptions it has about itself, even though those ideas it has attached itself to often rule its way of being. Left to its own devices, conceptualization within the individualized consciousness will eventually formulate an interior voice that conceives of itself as separate from other phenomena. It is a voice born through the tainted processing of an idea or experience which, in turn, becomes a memory that comes to sculpt an individualized being within the grand forms of a Being and Consciousness themselves.

CONCEPTS' EXPIRATION DATES

Simply stated, conceptions convolute reality. However, the convolution occurs mainly due to the outdated preeminence we give to concepts. Though, concepts, too — like anything else — have certain life cycles. Often, conceptions are useful for a time, but that time is always fleeting. Because conceptions are inaccurate views of reality, they can only last for a period, and when that period expires their utility expires along with it. However, what frequently ends up happening is that a certain kind of consciousness or mode of being becomes attached to a concept's utility and attempts to forcefully extend that utility past its actual usefulness. But this extension is usually accompanied with difficulties due to the fact that the utility itself was uniquely qualified because of its relation to the extenuating events around it; when those extenuating events change around a once relevant utility, the utility and the concept backing it become more or less obsolete by the same factors that once made them important. Naturally, a given thing is useful only in relation to its environment, and the environment is only as rich as the consciousness(es) which perceives and makes use of it. So, if a consciousness is attached to a mode which is outdated, it becomes corrupted by that attachment, and, thus, unable to fully interact with reality. As we will see, the potency of a consciousness is very much dependent on its ability to perceive reality. And reality is always pure, uninhibited, and openly accessible; whereas concepts are usually bias, influenced, and accessible only through specific avenues.

CONCEPTION'S BRIDGE TO NOWHERE

Though, the precise intention of a concept itself is often that it is an attempt to build a bridge to a truth. That is to say that concepts are often attempts to attain reality. When a location is unattainable, one must construct a bridge in order to reach it. Yet, within the realm of conceptual ideology, we often supplant the reality with the bridge, overemphasizing our abilities to cross that bridge while disregarding where it is that we're led to. After all, bridges are only constructions. It is the reality that is the natural location that the bridge was built for in the first place. So, that conceptual bridge becomes a way to interact with a reality we cannot readily access. However, one of conception's hypnotic tricks is that if a piece of reality seemed to have been gained through the use of a concept, a consciousness will be tempted to apply it over and over again in various other arenas — often to diminishing successes. But the problem seems to be that our fear of mystery often trumps our willingness to nakedly rendezvous with it. So, we stay encamped on the safety of the bridge where we can trace a line directly back to our own patterns of thought and mistake those patterns — those bridges — for the location we were attempting to obtain in the first place. The problem is that our humanity is built on bridge after bridge, seldom resting on the supports of a direct interaction with the reality the bridges attempt to deliver us to.

This degree of departure denotes the danger of conception: we use concepts, ideas, and a host of other conceptualized tools to interpret the world. But the interpretation is not the exact translation, just as the image we hold of a thing is not the reality. And yet we use the interpretation (an interpretation which is limited due to our limited abilities to observe) as the fact, compiling these so-called facts into laudable statements about actuality. The example of the marine biologist can be put to further use here: as a humanity, we gain our knowledge about sea-life from the field of marine biology. The field of marine biology is sustained by marine biologists. Marine biologists inform the general human consciousness about sea-life, yet the *study of* fish and the *actuality of being* a fish are two very different things. One would never say that one has a precise handle on the life of a fish simply by studying it. And yet, this is what we do with almost every aspect of what we consider to be knowledge of reality: we are given interpretations about various things by so-called experts, or from antiquity, and from those interpretations we formulate an understanding about a category. But if we are merely gaining our knowledge from others' comprehensions, we are removed from that information by several degrees, and the knowledge we take for granted as truth and a part of our understanding about humanity's relationship to the world is unverified by the individual. While this does not necessarily make specific types of knowledge untrue, at the same time it doesn't mean that we should wholeheartedly believe in what is given to us simply because we are taught a certain thing. Of course, we gain knowledge or learn a way of being by using interpretations from nuggets of information we allude to as "facts" given to us by experts in various fields or from history or a culture or system, and we build upon this knowledge base until we have comprised an understanding about a certain thing or cultivate a way in which we behave with an entity or in a particular circumstance. Of course, the problem is that if any of those "facts" given to us are not accurate — even by the smallest of degrees — then our relationship to the world becomes diametrically skewed. And just as dangerously, if certain ways of being are impressed upon us, these impressions leave little room for our truest selves to interact with reality on our own terms. And there is nothing worse than to lose one's individuality to the conformities of a culture.

HUMANITY'S TWISTED PREFERENCE FOR CONCEPTUALIZATION

The problem with knowledge at a degree is that there is no interaction, no direct experience or "being with" — only the abstracted distance from. And the abstraction then takes the place of the "being with", creating a sort of phantom reality. And yet, although we have not actually trained our conscious towards being able to decipher it, reality *is* with us. Like so much natural phenomena that we are unequipped to detect, what *is* encircles and sustains us without our knowing. Still, we rely on the conception because we can relate *to* it vis-à-vis our creation *of* it. But we trust in our own abilities as if they were uncorrupted, unbiased, objective, and directly dialed into reality.

The preference of conception is understandable, however: thought can generate an exact and traceable pathway back into itself, whereas reality often seems to leave us lost in an unrequited wilderness; however, the irony here is that reality only appears to us as mysterious and unrequited because the human consciousness has set itself up to compute and comprehend through the utility of thought. So, when faced with a choice, it is easy to see why we so often opt for the comforts provided by conceptualization: after all, concepts were constructed by the human consciousness, whereas reality's origins seem vastly more opaque. But again, in that same irony, because of conceptualization, we have become so detached from reality that *what is* has morphed into a mystery, and conception has become our perfunctory safe haven. Conception in relationship to humanity operates like an abusive guardian: it physically, emotionally, and psychologically exploits its children while at the same time providing for them a home. So, humanity has come not only to count on conception, but to love it as well. In our innocence we know nothing else.

THE ILLUSORY FORTIFICATION OF IDENTITY

For better or for worse, conceptualization and human consciousness have become one and the same. Through our own ideological creations, we have become gods and masters of self-created universes. In a morose codependence, conception gives humanity the very thing it craves most: an operating system by which to navigate through phenomena. And although the side effects of this operating system creates for us a vast amount of difficulty given that it requires the user to pay homage to the buffer rather than engage directly with the thing itself, from our most infantile stages of life we are taught to build upon and strengthen these buffers even though they are the cause of all the division and separation we encounter. And yet, we cannot imagine ourselves without them, for our entire world is predicated on the sturdiness of their structuring.

Of course, one of conception's most powerful seductions is that it gives its user a misguided comprehension of its *identity*. And though identities in and of themselves have a great number of benefits, they become extraordinarily dangerous when usurped by anything other than the inner nature of the individual. Identities are singular fortifications standing out against Otherness. Within an identity, a safe space is created within the world of apparent Otherness — a place where an individual can locate one's self amongst the mysteries of that which seems external. Of course, it is actually the concept that creates the identity as we have come to know it. And while our current understanding of ourselves is that we are born as individual beings, the actuality is what we have come to recognize as "individual" itself is merely another concept which has been concretized by a litany of ideas passed on from generation to generation.

We have taken this idea of a separate individual self so far that we have come to count on our mirage-like identities to survive. However, when a thing is constructed as something which inherently stands out against all other Being, to constantly struggle against that otherness is a natural part of its existence. That which, by its very nature, is viewed as independent *of* will continuously wreak havoc on nearly every aspect of its own existence. Identity, by its own construction, must be in some way combative. The singular, self-sustained identity is an isolated existence, and from its own viewpoint must be opposed to all that it encounters, operating against Otherness at a distance or degree. Therefore, identity and conception make excellent allies. Conception creates the conceptor, and the conceptor upholds the conception. The crime is perfect. Human consciousness and conception become the same thing. And given that the isolated identity sees itself as separate *from*, it naturally aims to reconnect *to* through a series of attempts to become, to know, to obtain, to possess, or to gain. The ego continually strives for more, creating voids within its own being and filling them with conceptual unrealities.

AN INITIAL PLAN OF ATTACK: CONQUEST BY DIVISION

We are so imbued with conception that even to extract ourselves from it and speak about it cogently is a difficult task. Again, though abundant, conception is elusive precisely because it has saturated itself into our very mode of being. To pinpoint it down to a corner where we can examine it at large is mostly an impossibility, and these initial pages are filled with vague notions and nondescript generalizations of a shoddy, cobbled-together picture of a subject too immense to capture in an accurate way. The army of conception is so forceful that we cannot take it head-on and hope to overrun it. But the best way to defeat a unified force is to first become intimately aware of every component of its nature — to observe, recognize, and acknowledge it as it is.

And when the time is right to strike, an opponent never confronts a powerful enemy head to head but must always seek to first divide it up. Through segregating the whole of conception, we will be able to better see how every facet of it has come to prey upon our lives. Therefore, after a careful examination of the enemy's army and its various regiments, a list of its numerous components and attributes has been constructed so that we may face this opponent not in its totality, but battle by battle, inch by inch. The enemies on that list are many, but they generally include: language, beliefs, institutions, patterns, cultures, traditions, systems, influence, power, control, emotion, the want to become, self-desire, possession, accumulation and attachment, the development of an isolated ego or general isolation and individuality, doubt or mistrust, descent and revolt, a misunderstanding of imagery and phenomena, incomplete information processing, formalized education, conflict, separation, division, otherness, tools, technology, the abuse of science, religion, dogma, authoritative power and control, emotion, abandonment, loneliness, powerlessness, meaninglessness, uncertainty, fear, anxiety, violence, competition, our current understanding of time and temporality, and the current notion of subject / object relations. All of these articles woven together come to represent a loose sum-total of the conceptual cloak. And when diluted into various sectors — like any army — they become weaker and less formidable. So, we will go after them point by point.

RECLAIMING THE THRONE
OF HUMAN POWER

Although we have deemed this war one of philosophy, to say that it is a war of thought, however, is incorrect: thought — as it is currently carried out within our individualized consciousnesses — is what we fight against (at least, as much as we are able to do so without engulfing ourselves in our own friendly fire). The term "thought", however, is much too narrow and much too short-sighted for our campaign. Thought alone does not stir reality; only action can do this. And this is a war of action — but not the kind of action which supplants one happening with another, or swaps out one government for another, or one idea for another. Our war is comprised of the kind of action which will radically change our consciousness and the kind of being it allows for if followed through to its successful conclusion. This is a war for an actual, tangibly different way of being human. Our resurgence is a way back toward our originality — back to the throne of human power — so that we can put a halt once and for all on the unending quest to become, and have the power and freedom to simply *be,* and, what's more, to be content with that being.

This quest is an enormous undertaking. But the duty of a General is to ready his troops for battle and to instill faith within his ranks. And while it is true that conception's power seems limitless at times, this lies in part due to the fact that it is so well hidden and entrenched behind our lines. So that is why we, by our mere rallying to fight, have already won this war. Even if our mission falls short, even if we become a casualty of this uprising, the action itself against that which consumes us — no matter how initially successful — is a victorious one. For, the sheer exposure of the enemy to those it enslaves is a monumental triumph. And it will only be a matter of time — so long as that recognition continues on — until the army which stands against us snivels before us.

HUMANITY'S DISTANT
RELATIONSHIP TO TRUTH

Humanity's search for truth only highlights our distance from it. So, the question we must ask ourselves is, why are we searching for truth in the first place? Why must we continually seek knowledge *of*? And why do the mysteries of the world keep themselves so hidden from us?

Paradoxically, however, truth is not a thing to be discovered: truth already *is*. It is only *we* who discover, and we do so because of our previously described fallen, misguided consciousness. Our history books are prime examples of this kind of false attribution: most say that a certain person discovered a scientific principle, or that an explorer discovered a certain area. Though, of course, these "discovered" things were already there — it was merely that humanity had been previously been operating at a distance from these exact realities. More accurately, these are not "discoveries" so much as they are bridges between humanity and mystery. The truth or the reality already exists; it is we who reach for it. But we have made reality a faraway land. Though, truth needs no intermediary, no formula, no system, no education, no dogma, and certainly no idea. Nothing needs discovering; we needn't learn or become something. In reality, there is nothing to attain, nothing to do.

Our war is a realignment of consciousness as it currently exists. Ad nauseam, the mind that we have come to know as the individualized human consciousness is a formulation of its own workings, and it has built itself through the haze of its own concepts and inartful stabs at reality. How individualized consciousness relates to concepts and how it relates to reality are two very different operations. An individualized consciousness relates back to its own self-constructions and builds upon them in a way in which it can comprehend and work with, creating its own language, methodology, and process. The operations of consciousness takes from what it perceives, but the perceiving is incomplete because of this continual inward turning toward its own limited devices. The conscientious experience with reality, however, is a totally different process altogether; for, the relationship between Consciousness and reality are what truly *is*: both the grand form and the individualized consciousness join together with *what is* and compose each other in an unending double reflection, creating and sustaining one another. And when a free mind freed of the inhibitions of conceptualization deals directly with reality, then what we think of as an individual mind and a reality of any scale become a singularized, unified action; that is, Consciousness and reality become one thing; and the individualized consciousness and the reality operate indistinguishably from one another in a solidified movement.

For the uninhibited mind, reality is simply present; it is not a thing to be apprehended through an outside vehicle. Reality is potential; and within that potential there is unlimited freedom. Further, reality is that which realizes the potential of Being. Concepts, however, are unrealities. They are ideas we have about anything at all. And, again, the idea is not the thing itself, but it is always removed at a degree from the thing which it idealizes.

CONCEPTS MAKE IT IMPOSSIBLE FOR A CONSCIOUSNESS TO TRULY EVOLVE

Our war can only be won if our enemy's ubiquitous abilities to hide in plain sight are exposed. The strategic tactics of conceptualization are merciless because they play on the individual's subjectivity, creating sympathies and bias within the subject where none previously existed. As both subjects and individuals, we have hopes and fears, wills and weaknesses — which is precisely what our adversary inflates and preys upon, like a farmer fattening a lamb for slaughter. That we cling to subjectivity so ferociously gives conceptualization all the more fodder to use against us. But we know of nothing else to do; so, often we feel that we have only ourselves as an ally in this war, operating as a lone soldier in an army of one. Though, the weaponry of subjectivity is ripe to be reforged. And once subjectivity is rebranded and fingered as the primary vehicle of conception itself, it will come under a similar fate. Subjectivity, after all, is simply a matter of orientation. When the orientation is turned toward another vantage point the perspective changes; but here, also, perspective is an orientation of a subjective entity.

Yet, under a consciousness controlled by conceptualization, nearly everything considered a so-called advancement of humanity is nothing more than some sort of shuffling of a position, or a retooling of our own outdated machinery. For, in a conceptualized mind, there is no real change of consciousness, but only a rotating of different concepts. This lack of true advancement and progress is evident everywhere from our most highly organized mass functions such as business and government, to our most basic human behaviors. For, in the end, we are motivated by our conceptions; this is due to the fact that motivation comes from a cocktail of our basic primal urges combined with our beliefs about ourselves and the world we live in. And, in fact, our primality itself is guided by the consciousness that fosters it. After all, evolution is slow to nonexistent if all that changes within the collective consciousness are the concepts it nurtures. And this is the precise reason why, for generation after generation, we as human beings have not made any truly significant changes in how we go about the business of being human; we are still motivated by brute power, and, to a lesser degree, a lust for the basic reactions of our animalistic natures. However, those animalistic natures — like all the various modes of Being — are still governed by their consciousnesses. And it is the consciousness of a given being that determines its physical nature and relationship to the rest of the phenomena it perceives. Yet, when a being operates with and in reality, evolution can occur instantaneously.

TRUTH'S ETERNAL RELATION

Though the question remains: why do we as human beings continue to seek out truth? Or, the better question may well be: why do we need to seek out truth in the first place? Humanity almost always speaks about truth as something 'out there', or as though it is somehow beyond us — a place or understanding *of* that is as mysterious as it is elusive. And in order to obtain that place or thing we are currently detached from, we need a pathway or a means that might potentially bring us closer to that reality which resides beyond our acknowledgment. So, we invent methods and systems to better relate to the world as we are able to conceive of it. For, as we see it, there is a gulf — an unknown element beyond us — so we build a bridge to breach the gap. We search, and yet, ironically enough, we seldom ask why it is that we need to search in the first place. Why is 'the unknown' some dark cloud that looms over every facet of our being? After all, it seems that human being is the only being continually at odds with its environment. So, it appears that we seek out of disharmony. After all, every action comes down to motive, and motive is always the child of need — or worse, the child of want. And it appears that it is our wanton need that fuels our search for this apparent truth behind ourselves.

Though, our philosophical war is one which seeks to destroy the need for any such bridge to truth. By its conclusion we hope to have opened up the direct channels which would allow for us to commune fluently with reality and dispense with the intermediaries, middlemen, and old-world systems that have put blockades between the individual and the actual for as long as we as human beings can remember. Candidly, this is a war to regain a direct relationship with reality as it is. It is an attempt to recapture simple being. For, in such simplicity, reality and the life it spawns is eternal. But in our current mode of continual seeking, we encounter only a continual attempt at becoming, and the presence of any sort of *being with* continually eludes us.

Yet, in this joining to and staying with that which actually *is,* we gain a harmonious relationship with reality and truth, and, in fact, live as truth itself. And through this reconnection to truth we are rejoined to something beyond our mere individuality: we are connected to that which exists beyond conception; and because of these broken conceptual bonds we are able to live in a space beyond our myopic notions of time and temporality and can coexist with truth's eternality.

So, our fight is one of and for life eternal; but it is not the mere notions of the eternality of religious afterlife or otherworldly rejuvenation: it is the real happening of actual, timeless perpetuation. Through the successful victory of this struggle we will defeat death in a way all religion has striven for yet failed to do. Our eternality is not a vision, it is not a story from an ancient tradition, or a time and place yet to come: it is a living, receptive happening unfolding with and for us.

A PHILOSOPHICAL WAR

Conceptions, systems, technological advancement — while, again, necessary in the way the drug is necessary to the addict — are our attempts to interact with an already skewed version of reality; and we must persist in these attempts so long as reality remains to us opaque. And, for better or worse, in a somewhat perverse turn towards conceptualization, systems have become our best attempts to interact with an obscured reality that always seems to be at a distance from us.

But what if we were to bypass the distractions? What if we pierced the heart of the issue, capturing the commander of the opposing forces? All the other questions, all the other sciences and systems and rationales would instantly become ancillary battles on the periphery of this, the one true war.

Our war is fought on the road back to ourselves; its struggle is to recapitulate our very being as one fulfilled by its own human purposes. It is a war more real and more devastating than any battle fought with material weapons and armies: for those material incarnations are only possible with the inception and the acceptance of the conceptualized ways we have chosen to implement throughout the courses of our human lives. And though the entirety of this work is written as something of a performance, the reality of its weaponry is more effectual than any of material warfare. This is a battle for humanity itself; it is a battle for human being, for Consciousness, for our hearts and the many beautiful qualities of human nature that are often so overshadowed by the barrage of injustices brought about by the ungracious acts of its occupying forces. In the most real way possible, this is the war to end all war; because, without our victorious completion of this struggle, war as we know it will continue. And though our offensive here takes place through metaphysics, it does so because there is truly no other way to fight. We cannot raise up a physical army against conception. We cannot shoot down ideology with missiles launched from a military post. So, we fight here, on its terms, with its weapons of idea and language, with a philosophy that seeks to end philosophies as we have come to know and endure them. Once we engage our opponent in the proper way, an inevitable victory will follow; because conception's fortifications are frail, its armor porous, and all its perceived strongholds a mirage — all surface without substance.

In our fighting, however, we need to comport ourselves with the delicacy and acumen of a strategic and purposeful force. This is dignified combat, and our fighting needs to be reflectively honorable. It is a civil war within ourselves, and it manifests in many unfortunate faces; it will arise and oppose us in the forms of the things we have been taught to honor and respect, and its most ardent commanders will often be people we love and admire dearly; which is precisely why we must execute our objectives with mindfulness and tact. So many of the things we will be fighting against are as much a part of us as we are of them. But there, in conception's stranglehold, also lies its inevitable downfall and its gift to us. Through its occupation, the seeds of our own liberation are sown: these things are us and we are them — a half-human, half-machine ranging in a robotic world that has glimmers of nature and humanity still seeping through the artifice. But we choose this war against the machinery, just as any war which is thrust upon us that endangers our lives. And we choose to fight; what follows here is that battle. This is a philosophical war. And we are in it.

CHAPTER III

THE ALLIES

VIM, VERITY,
& CONSCIOUSNESS

THE OBJECT OF WAR

Our war is a battle backwards. It is a search to regain. What it is we seek to recapture, however, is difficult to define. What's more is that our war's victory takes different forms for all of us; and yet, the essence of those various forms is the same for us all.

There is something that lies just below the surface of our lives — something so omnipresent to the nature of Being itself that we are often incapable of acknowledging its existence. And not only that, but this thing also saturates our own selves so pervasively that most of us are unable to identify it, much less distinguish it. And yet, it *does* exist both within and on the periphery of all Being and phenomena. However, when we attempt to focus on its presence it subtly recedes back into the general fold of the world. For, it is so commonplace that we think of it as unextraordinary; yet, it is the most fascinating presence imaginable.

The entire objective of our war is to harmonize with this thing. Other ideas and philosophies, beliefs, cultures, systems, institutions, and religions have given us vague glimpses of it — some even going so far as attempting to name its attributes or describe the entirety of its process. And through these many filters we have been given a generalized, popular understanding of what this thing is. Its importance for us lies not only in our understanding of *it*, but in the understanding it gives to *us*. The object of our war points to something beyond ourselves while at the same time allowing us to be what we are. What we seek not only makes our beings possible in form, but it brings flavor to existence by providing it with value and meaning which, in a grand orchestration, brings Being beyond itself and back to its original substantive essence.

Our ultimate prize is the source of all sources — neither attained nor unattained, for it is as far beyond the binary and the dialectic as it is beyond definition. Yet, due to the conceptualized natures of our minds it is precisely because it *is* beyond definition that we need to define it; for, as we shall soon see, language is where we begin to re-weaponize the forces of conceptualization for our own purposes. After all, how we speak about things leads to the ways in which we think and interact with them. Of course, the combination of language, thought, and action develop our relationship to any given thing; and it is the relation that is really the most vital factor of Being and phenomena. So, it will be extremely important for the conceptualized mind to implement language as a tool that helps liberate itself from the prison of ideology which it is currently confined within.

After all, relationships are all we truly possess as human beings: we are individual entities in constant conversation with all other modes of Being and force. But the most important relationship of all is the one we have with this all-encompassing entity. In fact, one might say that this thing is that which facilitates all the relationships within phenomena itself. Yet, however elusive it may seem, our war will beat away the murk and opaqueness of this near-phantom which lies beyond concept and definition, and, ironically enough, we will use conceptualization to draw it out of its gray shadow.

Our war is of such importance precisely because of its objective. For, regardless of who we are or what we do, once conceptualization has been put aside all that is left in its stead is the conclusion of this war. In fact, our very lives are this thing in motion, and those lives are constantly defined and given meaning through it. And not only that, but our lives aid mystery and help it to be by giving it action and expression.

The thing we seek, and the objective and conclusion of our war, is reality itself. It is life. It is pure Consciousness. It is the creative, the true, the actual — what *is*. We all seek it — all of us and at every moment — whether or not we are cognizant of it. And we seek it not in an act of selfishness, but together in the confluence of all Being. In acts seemingly small and large we help one another to achieve the starkness of this presence. For all of us come from it and return to it, only to act within it through our encounters with other Being and phenomena in between.

NOT "GOD"

However murky or aloof our war's objective may seem, it has been obscured solely by conceptualization and its many dark allies. Yet, historically, it has been the minds weighted most heavily by conceptualization that have attempted to give us pictures of reality through their labors of thought and ideology, dogma and a misshapen piety that is as useless as it is untrue. The product of these many balkish attempts to obtain an understanding about the nature of the universe and the Being it contains has resulted in a number of different words which name it directly. Many of these words are culturally or even scientifically colloquial, while others bear a more universally understood meaning.

The thing we seek has been called The Universal, The Supreme, HaShem, Abba, Brahman, Shangdi, Khora, Jehovah, Elohim, Parameshvar, Allah, Adonai, Jah, Krishna, Christ, Tao, Yahweh, Elah, Deus, Holy Spirit, The Almighty, The Light, The Way, and, most commonly, God. Whatever its name, it is among the oldest words in all of language. And as we shall examine at length, language is not only the most ancient, but also the most weaponized of all conceptualization's tools. This being so, it is easy to understand why one of the first arrows in the ideological quiver has so many poisons on its tip; and that is exactly why we must fight so vehemently to uncover its antidote.

The very word "god" itself is a mind game: like all too many linguistic symbols it is so commonly used that its definition is merely assumed. And it is this assumption that lands us in the deepest difficulties. For "god" is merely a word — nothing more. Like all words it points to something larger and beyond itself, and what that larger thing is is a great mystery which is unapproachable to the concept-laden consciousness. Being that our minds are structured around concepts and ideas about how things are, they cannot grasp this ultimate reality that the word "god" attempts to signify. Hence, even though many talk about "god" in the same way they might speak about something they tangibly interact with at an everyday level, they, at the same time, hold the concept of "god" to be a great mystery; when, in actuality, it is their own minds which propagate that mystery. Of course, it is we who have separated ourselves from what we call "god" through the adoption of concepts. And the only reality we now know is the mystery that that separation has left in its wake.

CONNECTING WITH
THE UNCONNECTABLE

However, to live shrouded in mystery is unnatural and, by definition alone, out of step with reality. In fact, our beings have become so estranged from what the word "god" signifies that nearly everything we do in our day to day lives acts as some kind of distraction or barrier to it. Of course, in reality, we are not separated by any degree from that which *is*; yet, again, our ideological minds trick us into believing that we are incapable of having a direct relationship *with* or complete understanding *of* any kind of ultimate truth; so, out of that trickery, further mysteries and lores are fabricated. It is at that point that the likes of philosophy and religion take up the banners of legitimacy and make their plays at filling up an existential void within our beings. However, our reliance on those teachings has often led us further from the truth rather than closer to it. For, nothing ever truly progressed by following a pattern precisely. Nor was anything ever deeply comprehended by merely being taught *at*; but it is only when we participate *with* and engage *in* that we can ever actually become melded so fully to the experience that we can learn from it in earnest. Understanding this, we can likewise comprehend the need to go beyond the previous pattern in order to move forward in a significant way. However, these dialogues and attempts at evolution require the active participation of the individual, not the mindless servitude professed by the modern teachings of formal education or any number of various religious practices. And through this active participation we help to influence and progress not only a practice, but also ourselves along with it.

For, our hope as human beings is constantly to connect. We wish to seek attainment and fulfilment *of* something — in fact, anything — as if we are not quite whole in our beings. The mystery which looms so pervasively within us is so great that we shun it by going down the rabbit hole of a daily routine, occasionally surfacing only to set our sights on meaningless entertainments. We have become preoccupied with any number of distractions and pay no attention to the deeper truths of our lives — talking and acting around these axioms as if they were too much for us to carry, and that we were fools to even make the attempt.

The mystery is greater than us . . . . . . Or so we think. And we stammer within a mind geared towards nothing because we have been subtly instructed to do so. We are taught to ruminate deeply on those things which are of utter inconsequence. And through those meaningless pursuits we somehow attempt to gain a connection to that missing piece beyond ourselves. However, of course, no connection can ever be reached; it is a bridge to nowhere — a fool's errand, and we are the stewards and glad practitioners of the task.

ABANDONING THE WORD "GOD"

But we are not willingly at folly: being that we have been taught no other way to bond, we seek an avenue — however meek and ill-suited it might be. After all, we have encountered very few things that have shown us a true way to connect.

Where there should be general acceptance, we espouse bias. Where there could be understanding and connection, there are lashes of violence and fear. And until we can rid our minds of the tumors of conception there will be no room for the kind of sight required for the discernment of truth, honesty, and a capacity for the attainment of an ultimate reality so undeniable that we cannot help but immediately come into its light.

With this in mind, we need to understand how misinterpreted (and because of that misinterpretation, divisive) the word "god" is and has been throughout history. And, for our purposes, because of this divisiveness, it gives us little recourse other than to strike the word "god" from language completely. Doing so will grant us a fresh slate on which to build a new conscientiousness capable of entering into a true connection with that which is real and undeniably present, as opposed to a distant, outdated idea about a being whose qualities, attributes, and even existence are continually debated.

Not only this, but the word "god" should be stricken from language because the idea of the word has no basis in our experience. Although, in everyday language it is most often used when speaking about its will (for example, when a disaster strikes, many of the faithful claim it to be "God's will"), what the word "god" points to has very little to do with the reality of its existence; or, as we shall also see, it is often only half of the equation. The "god" most often alluded to or invoked is one of legend, myth, and old books; its presence in the modern era is not adequately given due outside of an all-too quickly shrinking and impotent circle. The old, commonly referred to "god" is dead;[25] however, it is our objective here in this war to resurrect it. We need to comprehend it for what it is; and what it is is nothing like the "god" whose attributes, motives, and existence is questioned; that "god" is just a word attached to an idea. That "god" has long abandoned us. However, there *is* something present and active in the world, but, again, it is nothing like the "god" generally spoken about from the pulpit......But there is *something*. And what it is needs to be revitalized in our minds; only then can its true power and promise be evoked.

REMOVING THE CONCEPT OF "GOD"

One of the most important things we will fight for in this war is to expel the misidentification and misnomer of the reality that the word "god" only points to. What this thing that language flaps a wayward tongue towards is much deeper and certainly more real and omnipresent than has ever been revealed by any religion, mysticism, or spirituality. But our war will expose the hypocrisy of the concept of the word "god" and its assumed understanding by shutting down the word altogether. By striking "god" in language we play conception at its own game and remove the thought from our minds. And this simple act shows us just how concept-ridden our minds are: for, if there is not a word which names the thing, can our minds construct a traditional thought about the unnamed? We might well find

---

[25] The concept that "God is dead" is one made famous by German philosopher Friedrich Nietzsche's 19th century work, "Thus Spoke Zarathustra". Nietzsche's main point was that modernity's understanding of the world has basically replaced the classical notion of or need for God.

that by merely removing the name we lance a boil that has poxed our thinking from the first.

Because, the word "god" only serves to confuse us: it gives us old notions handed down from a thousand generations of concept-ridden pseudo-comprehension about what the word actually means. And yet, what very little we *have* come to know of this word we attempt to use as if it pointed to something in the basis of our existential lives such as a "tree" or the color "blue". Of course, even in these examples, when one person says "tree" another who hears the word might have a very different idea and experience with what a "tree" is: that is, the person who said the word might be thinking of an oak, while the person who hears the word might think of a Bansi; and while they may be scientifically classified under the same relative genus, the "trees" are two very different realities in almost every conceivable way. So, we can understand where so much uncertainty might arise from tossing around such an abstracted word as "god". Therefore, in order to make any advances in this war or our lives in general, that word and any previous notions we had of it must be done away with for good.

"GOD" AND REALITY

Furthermore, we needn't speak about "god" in order to obtain reality. The word "god" — because it is so laden with the heaviest and most burdened belief system ever constructed — skews our comprehension about what we witness in our own lives and the relationships we have to other phenomena. The only way to be an actual, unobstructed witness to ourselves and the lives which surround us is to do away with the thoughts and ideas that have been given to us about what the word "god" signifies. Because of language's corruption, the most beautiful and simple reality has become a cesspool of ideological pollution. If we could rid the human consciousness of the ideas built up within it about what "god" supposedly is, then it may become possible to obtain not only a cerebral comprehension of a deeper reality, but to have an actual experience with it. And, in what may be the ultimate irony, it is only then that we might be able to understand a kind of being akin to what the current use of the word "god" attempts to convey.

Although, in nearly every culture and religion the word "god" has some connotation of an ultimate truth, in order to obtain such a truth, we must recalibrate our perspectives — which often means stripping away many of the trappings of both culture and religion.

All too frequently, however, we become weighted down by debates about what the word "god" points to and how such an existence lines up with our observable universe. Of course, the cosmic joke remains that even if the kind of being the current word "god" points to *does* exist, we would never be able to apprehend it given the conceptually sluggish natures of our current minds. Therefore, what needs to happen in order to start anew is to take all the comparisons between Vishnu and Raah, Jehovah and Jesus, Allah and Buddha, and put them aside. For, although these figures have beautiful and prominent places in the hearts of various histories, they can only lead us so far; ultimately it is up to us to take the final lunge into *what is* and maintain our existence within it. And although these various interpretations of the word "god" might be helpful guides towards that end, they ultimately can only lead us to the precipice of reality; it is we ourselves that must cross into the state of an actuality which is present and alive — whereas these many cultural and religious figures are neither. Therefore, it is not so much that "god" itself is dead, but more so that the notions we had of it were never truly alive to begin with.

So, again, if we could rid ourselves of this notion of the meaning and attributes of all the many concepts of the word "god" and merely focus on the simple, naked reality of what is, then we would finally have a clear pathway which might at long last grant us a relationship with what the classical notion of the word "god" offers us. So, here in our war we are not rallying behind the notion of "god": we are rallying behind an actual truth — free and clear of any attachments given to us by history. And our truth is undeniable because there are no ideas attached to it, but only the presentism of the interaction between observer and observed, between Being and phenomena, spirit and Consciousness. We will tell no tales, spin no stories, and harken to no ancient book: for truth which is alive in the here and now does not reside in any of these spaces. Let others seek out a notion of what the word "god" points to; but as soon as they begin to search, they are already off course: for, reality needs no finding, nor would it be reality if it did. So, this so-called "god" of the lazy, conceptual mind is best left alone or to those who pride themselves in plagiarizing the ideas of their ancestors.

Here in our war, we seek only reality. Of course, however, when one is in step with actuality, that is all there is; no searching for a "god" (or anything else) is needed. Again, through searching we are lost. The thing that conceptualization attempts to label as "god" is not something which necessarily needs to be sought out; it is already present. (Again, if it were not present already it would not be a reality of any kind, much less the ultimate reality.) Therefore, the kind of presence we are attempting to reconnect with by shedding the weights of concepts leaves us seeking and desiring nothing. Yet, the notion of "god" given through religions has many rules and can only be attained through a strict diet of ritual, practice, and a particular state of mind.

However, again, when in the presence of reality there is nothing one needs. And this is the true goal of all individual being: to peacefully do away with itself and be swept up into the tide of all creation so that it directly reconnects with all other Being. And in this connection, individual being both loses itself and at the same time gains all other Being. Again, this is the aim: to be directed into letting go of the self so that we might gain the world. And we must follow this path if we are to attain reality in a concept-stricken dimension. We have the opportunity to attain reality — and thus all things — if we loosen our grips on the ideas about the selves we have created. After all, the only thing necessary in our war and in our lives is to attain reality and truth, and this can only be done if we shed the layers of concepts that allegedly compose our identities. For, the identity is the starting point of all our relations, and, being so, it must also be redefined for there to be a true relationship with reality.

A NEW POWER

Of course, nearly every organization and institution we have in our ideologically-based society revolves around the underlying notion of power. Many religions, cultures, philosophies, and societal norms have popularized the idea that the attainment of power is the pinnacle of existence. Not surprisingly, the kind of power glamorized through the lenses of these structures is the one which enables its procurer to produce an intended effect upon a given circumstance or the world at large. Of course, the difficulty with producing effects is that often the wielder is unable to ultimately control the consequences, and once those effects are put into motion, more and more effects must be instantiated in order for the original effect to continue on. Thus, that which is allegedly powerful in the traditional understanding of power must constantly be maintained — and such upkeep takes a great deal of resources and energy (which, of course, are usually only garnered through the obtaining of greater and greater powers, all of which keep the nasty cycle of the so-called power struggle alive and well).

But the kind of power we seek is altogether different from the power structures we have become accustomed to. Furthermore, the power our war connects us with is a kind of ability that most never even think to seek out; and, even if they did, their minds would be so conceptually burdened that they would have little hope of attaining it.[26] The power the conclusion of our war affords, however, will catapult us into a realm vastly beyond the back-and-forth struggle we witness in the known scramble for power and success. For, once achieved, the power our war's victory brings to us needs no maintenance; and furthermore, once possessed it is impossible to lose. Again, what lies at the conclusion of this war is the

---

[26] It should be noted here that we do not wish to "attain" anything in the traditional sense; that is, we do not seek to "capture" something. More accurately, attainment here means to enjoy a coexistence *with*.

attainment of simplistic reality. And it is our task to understand this reality and get a clear notion of what it is[27] and how we might best come into its graces.

Of course, our war's path and purpose is the manual which guides us. And yet, at the same time there is ultimately nothing to attain; what is of greater importance is that we let go of those things that have attached themselves to us (or, just as likely, we to them). And we are only able to shed these entanglements when we let go of the conceptions which bind our minds to further ideologies in a never-ending cycle of attainment and attachment *to*. Of course, when we let go of the plaques that build within our consciousness we can step back and be observers in our own lives, acting as vanguards of universal forces and animated muses for the cosmos. And in this realization a great yet subtle force flows through our souls and grants us the freedom of a full and complete life.

Once again, the interesting thing about the power our victory gains us is that it is unlike "power" as we have come to understand it. (Of course, this makes sense being that our traditional ways of thought are made possible to us through the conventions of conceptualization.) The power we experience

---

[27] We have, quite intentionally, strayed away from giving a complete and definitive definition of "reality" so that we might freely explore it as opposed to defining it and then attempting to fit whatever we say about it into said definition. However, if we must give it a definition, we might just say that reality is what *is*. Of course, what *is* is largely determined by the perceiver. Though, as we have already pointed out: concepts are only given realities by the perceiver and have no existence outside of those perceptions. This would indicate that concepts are tethered to the individualized consciousness (or a group of consciousnesses), while ultimate realities are bound more so to the grand form of Consciousness; that is to say that concepts could not survive unless they were constantly upkept by an individualized consciousness (or group of consciousnesses), whereas reality (or realities) would not need an individualized consciousness in order to maintain being.

when shedding the many burdens of our minds allows us an inconspicuous, yet altogether immense energy; this happens because, unlike with the usual attributes of conventional power, this force is wholly uncompetitive: in fact, it is precisely because of its low-lying nature that it becomes the greatest of all catalysts. This is a power that exists in servitude to all other Being. And it is in its servitude that it becomes the ruler. For this power is not something taken from another only to be usurped again: it is a power that is produced when one joins together with actuality and bonds to the eternality of the truths it uncovers from doing so. It is not a power obtained through conquest, but one rewarded through observation, contemplation, and, finally, connection — which leads one into the grand hall of comprehension. And more than anything else, it is this connection and the comprehension which comes from it that at long last allows our fullest, most natural being to come forth, while at the same time opening the door for Being itself to harmoniously exist with and within us.

THE MIRAGE OF CHOICE

Of course, all of conception's workings have served to inhibit the natural synergistic relationship between reality and the self. And herein lies the true danger of conceptualization: it looks to replace reality by making it into an alternative narrative — something that can be chosen as opposed to that which is undeniable. And by merely presenting a choice between reality and conception, ideology gains a great victory: for, if we are made to stutter and balk at what *is* — even if we eventually choose the road which leads us to actuality the seeds of conception are planted in our minds, and we look twice at 'the real' until we begin to doubt it altogether; this is conception's game. And this being so, we must beat concepts at their own rules by identifying and measuring them against what is. After all, this sort of delusion only exists if we choose it; yet, by being aware of the influences and constructs of our own consciousness we will always be guided down reality's road. Because, our war is about the purification of our consciousness so that we are made aware that such a choice between concepts and reality does in fact exist. Of course, in the end, if such a consciousness is truly clean, the awareness of a choice only means that no real choice exists and that the only way of being is that which keeps with reality.

Unfortunately, whether or not we are aware of it, up to this point our consciousness has by and large chosen to structure itself using the raw materials of conceptualization. And through those choices we have distanced ourselves from the reality that ultimately sustains us, denying our truest, most ultimately powerful selves in the process. But what may be even more blasphemous and harmful — if we are to believe the rhetoric of the modern-day religions — is that we have continually chosen against what the word "god" points to. (Which is to say that we have chosen against what our modern concept of the being of what the word "god" points to.) For what this word indicates is an ultimate freedom of being. Yet, if we look at the modern religions, most of what emanates from their teachings and interpretations puts some kind of boundary or restraint on their practitioners. Therefore, we are either bound by those teachings, or those teachings view us as previously bound and the teaching itself is the attempt to free us. Either way, religion interacts with human being as a kind of being tethered to failure. However, this viewpoint is contradictory to what we would experience if we existed in a harmonious relationship with actuality.

Though, operating from the perspective that humanity is naturally at one with reality only to be pulled apart from it through conceptualization, the pathway towards what the word "god" indicates becomes much more simplistic than it could ever be under the guidance of a religious tenet. For, an alignment with actuality would give us a true comprehension of the way in which things are, and such a comprehension would give us a kind of freedom we could never hope to enjoy given the manner in which our consciousnesses currently process phenomena.

But this war — much like any war truly worth fighting within — is about regaining our freedom. And again, concepts take away that freedom by setting up the false scenery of choice. Although it seems paradoxical to say that choices are actually restraining, when operating under the sway of conceptualization it is always the choice which binds us: although there may be a multitude of options, if those options are tainted by a particular ideology, then, in the end, the only choice one makes is what flavor of philosophical poison is to be swallowed. Yet, when we operate in step with reality, the choice is so obvious that it renders all the other options moot. Of course, there are various ways of existing or operating *with* a given reality, but, ultimately, the choice eventually winds up giving the chooser access to a harmonious interaction *with*, or it leads one down the dark and deadly pathways of a conceptual wasteland.

Concepts and the mirage of choices they present give us the false impression of freedom. Yet, our freedom is akin to a prisoner choosing which wall of his cell to stare at. If we were truly free there would be no choice at all — and in that lack, there exists a purified freedom that carries us beyond the need for choice. This is where the states of contentment and acceptance rear themselves into our being for possibly the very first time: for, if we possess contentment and acceptance, options become nonfactors. In fact, though contentment and acceptance, choices break down and we are left with only the keys to true and everlasting freedoms. After all, if we are able to choicelessly accept a circumstance or being, contentment will naturally arise, and out of that contentment we will be birthed into a requited freedom.

And yet we think we are free to choose between a great many things: for one, we believe ourselves to be free to act, or at the very least think — even if those thoughts cannot be acted upon. But here again we are hoodwinked by ideology, for the actions we are left with are constrained by a great many circumstances, and our thoughts are handcuffed by the structures of our conceptualized minds. Indeed, we are enslaved by the many choices in front of us! Again, the only real choice we have is to select concepts or reality. But in order to choose correctly we must see the pervasiveness of concepts within our consciousness in the first place, and how they prey upon our good-natured innocence. We are at the least unaware, and at the most apathetic to this ideological prison we have volunteered to stay within. And if we were to suddenly realize our confinement, we would have little idea as to how to break out.

Of course, what *seems* and what *is* are two very different happenings. And there *is* something we can do — something we *can* choose — but we need to acknowledge its existence before we can act within its graces. And this is where we begin to reclaim our stake. This is the catalyst of the final battle. It is the key to unlocking not only our own existential prison, but to all the barriers between ourselves and truth.

PARTICIPATING WITH THE INDICATION

What muddies our prospects, however, is that we must meet conception on its own battlefield and use its primary tool, language, against it. Language, while being one of the most useful tools we have at our disposal, also has the capacity to vehemently handicap us. Language is the womb and graveyard of all modern human thought and action. But to fight this fire with a fire of our own we need to play conception's game and repurpose its weapons through the general reclaiming of language itself as a whole. And the first word we need to reclaim and redistribute is "god". The word "god" has become too heavy, too burdened with all the worst of concept's many ills. And yet, ironically, what the word "god" points to is the very thing the conclusion of our war achieves: that is, the word "god" is most often meant to be an ultimacy or pure reality that we as human beings are attempting to serve, work with, or in some way understand; the final object of our war is no different. However, somewhere along the way a wedge was thrown in-between ourselves and what the word "god" indicates: where, at one time, we were able to interact directly with the reality of this thing we now call "god", we became able to participate only with what the word indicated. Therefore, instead of participating with that thing itself, we could only interact with that which it left in its wake. So, like a philosophical golden calf, we began giving the *indication* superiority and priority over the *actuality* until we became so far removed that the only remnant left of the reality was the indication itself. And the indication has now been crumpled into a singular word with many different connotations — all of which point only to further mysteries while failing to delineate or concretize any discernible reality. Therefore, we must keep the end of our war in mind while at the same time discarding the common conceptual pathways which have disoriented us. However, where we blow out one trail, we will, at the same time, create a new, direct roadway.

THE NEW IS

Language is a wonderful tool, but, like any weapon, we need to utilize it carefully in order that we don't harm our own selves while doing so. At this point in time, the word "god" does nothing but indicate a universally common mystery to all humanity. The word "god" often confuses and separates us as human beings because of the many conceptualizations we have attached to it over the ages. Not only that, but because of these conceptual ties and demarcations, the word — like all words — can only serve as an indication of the greater reality it points to. Therefore, we must reiterate that it is time we discard it from our lexicon; by doing so we may be able to trick our conceptualized minds into interacting with what the word "god" can only infer to us. If we erase the word "god" from vernacular language, that language and the individual consciousnesses which support it are given a clean slate. Because commonly used words are already leashed by their prescribed definitions, new or repurposed words have the ability to open up a space within the colloquial vocabulary so that the reality which those new words point towards can be interacted with freshly and without the chains of their past definitions. After all, we act in the way we speak about things, and we speak in the way we think; that is, our thoughts are often given articulation through language and certain words within it, and those words carry with them various ideas which boil over to the actions which, along with our thoughts and speech, comprise our beings. So, if we can rid our language of a certain word, we may be able to reapproach what it had previously indicated and bring that indication into an actualized reality.

Therefore, we elect to attempt that maneuver first and foremost with the word "god", hereby expunging it from our language and replacing it with something more agile, flexible, and true to its indication. And the word we choose to replace "god" is "Verity".[28] Our hope is that the word "Verity" will allow us a direct interaction and participation *with*. Verity does not indicate: Verity *is what is*; and, being so, it is the perfect replacement for the word "god" — a word that, through several millennia of conceptualization, had become capable only of suggestion and indication.

With Verity we have something active and present; it is alive and its being is undeniable — or, rather, its presence is not up for debate. Verity *is* reality; it *is* existence, and it *is* nonexistence: it *is* whatever *is*. It has no dull edges or cloudy ambiguity, and yet, at the same time it is both without degree and of many degrees. It is the subject, object, and the relation.

---

[28] Of course, one can choose any word one might prefer so long as it allows the chooser a fresh perspective on whatever it was the word "god" of old language attempted to indicate.

Unlike the word "god" of old language, its attributes are not up for discussion: it exists bluntly — without apology or backspeak. Verity is energy, life, Consciousness, and spirit. It is the birthplace of all phenomena and the resting place of all action. It forms the form, exists as such a form, and gives power to its being. It *is* what *is*. In short, Verity is reality in the larger scope, and at the same time it is also the smaller happenings which compose that larger reality. It is the thing, the setting, and the interaction between the two. All things can be traced to it and are at the same time heading back towards it. If not wholly apparent with them all, Verity is just below the surface of every thought, emotion, action, and being. It is the happening and the consequence — a state, a form, and a metaphysical space.

And although all things come from and revert to it, Verity begins to die away where concepts lurk. Ad nauseam, concepts are ideas *about* — not direct interactions *with*. And being abstractions *of* reality, concepts pose *as* realities and trick consciousness into a perception of reality that is inaccurate and, thus, not a kind of being that exists *with* what is, but a befuddled being that operates at a distance *from* what is; and that is why we need to root out conceptualization as a primary process; because, to do otherwise is to invite a hazy version of consciousness to interact with pure reality; and when a hazy, conceptualized consciousness and Verity mingle, that fragmented mind pollutes reality by misinterpreting its own observations, and such a consciousness then slips further and further into a conceptual fog by acting upon those misinterpretations. However, if structured the proper way, Consciousness will begin to not only see Verity in all things, it will begin to see all things as mere forms of Verity itself.

And, as we shall come to understand shortly, the relationship that Consciousness has to reality is so intricate that it is of the utmost importance that we keep it as pristine as possible.

VERITY'S ETYMOLOGY

The word "Verity" comes from the prefix "ver", meaning "truth". Combined with the suffix of "ity" — which means a quality or state of being stemming from Middle English's "-ite", or old the French "-ité", and directly from Latin "-itatem" — the word comes to mean that which is true and undeniable, or the supreme and ultimate truth. One of the many useful things about the word is that its malleable meaning can be applied to something either phenomenological *or* a metaphysical condition. Either way, it cannot be stated enough that unlike what the word "God" of old language indicated, Verity's existence is undeniable. In fact, if it *were* deniable it would cease to be Verity. Also, being that the word means supreme and undeniable truth means that the word points to a grander happening beyond itself; that is, it points to truth as a process and a live being to be reckoned with in the here and now. Physical things which play out in the material, phenomenological world are kinds of verities — all of them pointing beyond themselves to something greater.[29] And here is where we begin to use conception against itself: whereas, in conceptualization, language uses words to point to things beyond themselves, we can now use individual

---

[29] More will be said about this in a section entitled "Nonjectivity" in a later volume of this work.

beings and events as phenomenological markers which indicate something beyond their own manifestations. Pure conception, however, is what we might call an "inverient": that which is removed from Verity by a degree or is totally devoid of it.

VERITY & NOTHING

Although verities are any and all things which exist, Verity itself is not without mystery. Yet, true to form, Verity's mystery is actually an illusion: Verity only appears mysterious because our conceptualized conscious states hinder us from comprehending it directly. Verity is always itself; that is, Verity is that which is real and actual. It is only conceptualization which keeps us from it. This being so, Verity remains all things, and yet, in our conceptualized states, it is not actually locatable.

Further adding to the apparent enigma, Verity is born out of that which is *not*; which is to say that while Verity itself is that which *is*, it is created by that which is no actual thing itself. *Nothing* creates Verity: Verity *is*. Which means (and is possibly easier to digest for our conceptualized minds) that Verity is created out of nothingness. Logically, that which *is* comes from that which is *not* and vice versa; it is the same with Verity. So, if someone were to ask where and how Verity is created, the answer is, quite literally, that it is created by nothing, from nothing, and it is that nothingness that sustains it and makes its existence a possibility. Nothingness gives rise to Verity's existence, and Verity, in turn, allows for nothingness. So, Verity has both being and simultaneously "has" nonbeing: it is both the manifestor and the manifest. And because Verity also "possesses" nonbeing, it is able to create Being; similarly, because of its capacity to create, maintain, and destroy in a continual cycle, it is clear that it both has form and can create form; of course, it is able to create form in the first place because it simultaneously has no form at all. And Verity, through nothingness, becomes all happening itself: it is that which gives and takes — the resting place of all things in thought, emotion, and form. It is what happens (even if that happening is nothing itself), and its happening — that is, reality in both its many individual manifests and the grand total of those manifests — cannot ultimately be argued or debated. And while Verity's degrees and features may be interpreted in various ways, its ultimacy and actuality are beyond all controversy.

VERITY IS WITHOUT
AN INDEPENDENT QUALITY

Verity is the action[30] and actor alike; and, furthermore, it is the relationship between the two. It is both the state which makes Being possible and the particularized form of Being itself. It is a movement, a power, and the force of and behind things. However, unlike our traditional notion of the word "God", Verity tends to escape the strict labels of quality and attribute; that is to say that Verity is both the attribute and the state which makes the attribute possible, and, therefore, is also that which stands against the attribute itself; whereas, for example, the classical notion of "God" is a being that is omnipotent,

---

[30] For further elaboration on how Verity operates as action, see the subsection on "Vim" below.

Verity could never be bogged down and labeled as having a particular characteristic without also speaking about all the surrounding circumstances which comprise the characteristic. Where biblical text may talk of "God" as being wrathful (that is, wrath is a particular character trait of the God of the old testament), we can only speak about Verity in terms of wrath itself: that is, we can only speak of the happening of "wrath" and its origin — both of which cannot be ascribed to a singular being which is separate from other kinds of Being.

It is here that Verity begins to open up one of the structures of language: language is a composite of singular words which each have a particular meaning. However, there are various words that have different meanings depending on their context; and, together with both the individualized meanings of the words combined with the context given to those words by the other words that surround it, the grand structure gives way to both a meaning, quality, and the joint effort of the micro and macro functions of the language itself. It is the same with Verity: there is no one being alone that is Verity; however, Verity has both micro and macro components which come together to create the reality of a given structure. Verity simply *is*. There is no being that is the alpha Verity which has components and attributes independent of all other Being — unlike the common notion of a "God".

VERITY AS A CONCEPT, & CONCEPTS AS POTENTIAL VERITIES

Of course, we do not only think of the old notion of "God" as a kind of being with certain attributes; we think of all things in this manner as well: we think of water as having various qualities in the exact same way that we think of a rock or an old man as having particular characteristics that compose their beings. Verity, however, is both the totality of existence and the singular beings and events within that larger existence. Therefore, for our conceptually saturated minds to grasp what exactly Verity is, we must approach Verity without a particular idea or notion, and experience the veritable happening or thing for itself alone. For what Verity is is the simplest of things; it is only the unpacking of it that becomes complicated to our fragmented and ideological minds. Verity itself, however, is easily identified and experienced; in fact, Verity is the basic and natural state of things and occurs constantly whether or not we are aware of it. What's more is that to be aware of Verity is to also be aware of our own selves and the relationship we have to Verity. And, again, there is nothing that must be done in order to attain it this awareness — unless, of course, the kind of consciousness we implement has been ransacked by conceptualization.

And yet, even concepts themselves have a modicum of Verity within them: for, after all, concepts are put into play by something that has a reality. And, if a concept gains traction, that concept could potentially carve out a niche for itself within the grand scheme of things and ultimately come to influence that larger scheme — a larger scheme which, being something that *is,* is, in fact, also Verity. So, all things — concepts included — have a degree of Verity within them.

However, it may be more accurate here to identify concepts as a kind of cancer within Verity: just because concepts have a degree of verience within them does not mean that, left to their own devices, they couldn't very well subsume, squash out, and eventually kill off Verity — or, at the very least, retard it. And this is the precise importance of our war: Verity is so real that all things are *within* it, are powered *by* it, and *become* it (or, more accurately, always have *been* it). Therefore, we must be very-very careful about what we generate, because those concoctions will eventually be our realities. So, Verity can be seen as a kind of genie in a bottle: it gives us whatever we wish for and attempt to conjure. Truly, all things are Verities — or, at the very least, could be said to have Verity within them. This is why we need not ultimately fret: Verity will eventually find itself again. However, we can do our part by allowing it to flow all the more easily by acknowledging and reinforcing it. Where we begin to stop-up Verity's natural flow is when we blur the lines of reality by having ideas about things and states which have no real weight outside of the thoughts we give to them. Again, Verity is that which is true, actual, and real — and not because we think of or observe it to be, but because it *is*. Of course, our actions can sometimes help to compose and define what Verity is and how it operates, which is why it is important to be open to an interaction with Verity without the bondage of the many processes of conceptualization.

THE PEBBLE & THE TREE

Aside from being the relation between various modes of Being, Verity also facilitates the setting for the relation. Again, Verity is not only the action and the actors, it is also the script, stage, setting, and play itself. Whatever *is* is Verity — whether that thing or state appears to the constructs of our minds as an individualized or overarching happening or being. Verity is as much the foundation of Being and phenomena as it is the undefinable and unattainable space between and surrounding it. Where nothing prevails, Verity also reigns. Therefore, again, Verity is both something and nothing all at once, and through its "nothingness" Verity can create Being and phenomena. (Remember that it is precisely because Verity does not have any singular or particularized being, quality, or relation that it is able to give rise to beings and relations.) Verity is the core, the very truth *of.* And by being this kind of essentiality and center of all things which both exist and at the same time do not exist, it is able to set up all relations and things — even nothing itself. By being that which undeniably *is* it facilitates all else — even its own destruction. By being completely open to all potentials, it sets up and contains all other realities within it and vice versa.

Verity, being ultimately true and apparent, is never undisclosed; one simply must know how to interact with it. In fact, it is even readily apparent in all phenomenological Being. Take a physical location — let's say, Claremont, California, for example: a location that is apart from Claremont is needed to make Claremont, which means that all the places we think of as disconnected from Claremont actually help to compose Claremont. That is to say that Chicago, Illinois, helps compose and define what and where Claremont is by *not being* Claremont. Claremont comes out of Chicago by standing against Chicago, just as Chicago comes out of Claremont by not being Claremont. Claremont is in Southern California; it is dry and warm, there are mountains on every side of it and it sits only a few miles from the greatness of the Pacific Ocean. Some two thousand miles to the Northeast sits Chicago — colder, flatter, flanked by Lake Michigan to its East and the once long-miled prairie to its west. These two places are what they are because they stand against one another. And yet, it is that opposition that allows each location to be contained *within* each location; what we perceive of as differences between various locations are the ingredients which serve to compose each location.

The same can be said of certain kinds of Being. For instance, a pebble is different from a tree according to our mind's perception. And yet, veritably speaking, for both the pebble and the tree to be what they are they need each other. We could not say that this is a pebble and that is a tree if there weren't other things in the world that were not pebbles and trees. The pebble cannot be itself unless it stands against the tree; the pebble needs the tree to make the pebble the pebble, which means that the tree is in the pebble and the pebble is in the tree. When the pebble is itself, it is already outside itself, and at the same time it is also the tree and everything else; that is, it is already whatever is not the pebble. Because, again, for the pebble to be a pebble it must come out of the tree and everything else; if the pebble did not contain in itself what is not itself, whatever is not the pebble could not come out of the pebble so as to make the pebble what it is. The pebble is the pebble only because of this veritable happening; and it is just as much a pebble as it is the tree; only our minds separate the two things. Phenomenological entities exist only because of this contradiction, and this contradiction comes out only when we attempt to logically place things into conceptual categories.[31]

---

[31] The example of the Pebble & The Tree is an extraction from a selected writing by D.T. Suzuki's, entitled, *"Existentialism, Pragmatism and Zen"*.

In a broader view, every phenomenological occurrence or being our minds perceive as "separate" from other beings or phenomena are actually needed to compose those other beings or phenomena; and they all need Verity — that thing which holds up their existence and gives them the reality they enjoy — to make them what they are. And, likewise, Verity comes out of all these things and is a part of all these things, just as all things come from Verity. One's very being, here and now, is currently standing at the genesis of all that is and is not; all things and events that have occurred in the past, will take place in the future, or are happening at this moment, originate from a present veritable occurrence.

Of course, in Verity there is no past or future: the labels of "past" and "future" imply distinctions that simply don't exist — distinctions of individual perceptions brought about by and through conceptualization. With Verity, there is only happening and perception *of* through being *with*; and this perception *of* and being *with* do not require linear time to unfold. For, everything is Verity, so there is really nothing to gain and nothing to do in order to gain it. And since nothing comes into being without it, all phenomena and Being is just Verity acting with and within itself. There are no events or beings which are separate from one another; everything is Verity; everything is, at base, the same. In this way, there is no true becoming — only the discoveries of various ways back to Verity. Everything is composed with and within everything else. Therefore, nothing really is: only Verity is. For, when all is broken down to its most basic element, Verity is the only thing that truly is. All things that are perceived as distinctive forms and happenings are simply different manifestations of the same single thing. But our limited perceptions, duped into conceptualization, distinguish everything from everything else. Yet, all things are really nothing more than Verity, and it is Verity that creates all things. And within every mode of being in the universe, Verity is there. It is calling us, within us. When we have a connection to Verity, what we think of as "truth" simultaneously appears. In fact, it's something known to us already; we just have to rediscover it — we have to listen to it. But it is there.

VIM

Verity is the fact, the reality. It is the thing and the non-thing from which Being and phenomena emerge and fall back into. Verity is the whole and the complete universe of Being, events, essence, and phenomena — just as it is also the individualized particulates of those happenings and existences. And yet, Verity possesses a power that activates and animates *it*. (Although, it could just as easily be said that Verity's state of being or nonbeing is responsible for the generation of this power.) This power that is both generated by Verity's existence and also sires and ushers Verity into being is not at all separate from Verity, as, of course, no thing is without Verity and vice versa. (Though, as with every process of the mind under conceptualization, it is all in the way the thing is perceived.) So, we might think of this thing as the product of Verity, or we may just as easily think of this thing as producing Verity; either way, the two are inextricably interconnected. For our purposes, we call this force of Verity "Vim": that which emanates from Verity, and also creates and animates it.

Vim is Verity's conduit. Vim is action — or, rather, it is the activity of Verity. It is the dynamic force in the realm of Being and phenomena. Vim is the energy that exists both within Verity itself as a whole and as all other events and individual beings within phenomena. If Verity is the thing, Vim is the energy it produces; and, just as easily, it could be said that if this power is activated, what it engenders is Verity.

If Verity is the body, Vim is its spirit. Vim labors through Verity's employ; that is to say that Verity is the reality that exists, and what it produces through its existence is Vim — which forms another kind of Verity and repeats the cycle. Analogously, if Verity were an engine, the power it produced would be Vim, and, through the generation and harnessing of that power (Vim), another engine (Verity) could be constructed so that the cycle might continue. So, again, Vim is the force of a given veritable happening. And Vim both produces Verity just as it can be said that Verity produces Vim. Indeed, Verity and Vim are really two sides of the same coin: there is no mislabeling or misinterpretation of either, as what we might think of as Verity could just as easily be called Vim and the other way around. Verity is Vim and Vim is Verity. But it is helpful to our conceptualized minds to have some definition of Vim and Verity so that we might see how they interplay to better understand the entirety of the events and beings they produce, sustain, and demolish.

So, Vim produces Being, events, and their subsequent phenomena, making them into realities (Verity). (That is, out of Verity as a whole, Vim creates a myriad of individual verities.) And after a certain expenditure of its particularized Vim, those beings and events then re-merge back into the whole of Verity from which they came. So, in Verity, all things have potential, and that potential is then actualized by Vim: Vim molds the potential into a manifestation. Again, if Verity is the motor, Vim is the energy created by its workings. Verity is the total song, while Vim represents the notes that compose and bring it together; one is difficult to locate without the other, and we could not really speak accurately of one without keeping in mind the other as well. After all, Vim's work allows Verity its existence, just as Verity's existence allows Vim to do its work.

VIM'S RELATIONALITY

The relationship between Vim and Verity might be best articulated by looking into our own beings. If we attempt to define ourselves, we come up against a curious task: where do we begin? (Or, for that matter, where do we end?) Are we merely our physical traits? Surely not. But, neither can we say that we are only our mental capacities. Of course, if we were to say that we are a combination of both our physical and mental beings and attributes, this does not take into account our emotions or our experiences, or our relationships, or things we care for, or our beliefs, our fears, our hopes, and. so on and so forth. And even if we were to combine all these things, it would not be accurate to point to the totality of our perceived self and label it as something individual, per se; for, all of those attributes — all of those physical and mental capacities and their subsequent beliefs and experiences and emotions — all have relationships with other kinds of Being and phenomena that come to compose them; so, it would be inaccurate to say that there is an entity that is completely "individual" from the others. Just as it is with the pebble and the tree: all those things we perceive of as external to who we are as individuals serve to shape the idea we have of the self. And yet, we absolutely do understand ourselves to have an identity that exists apart from other kinds of Being.

Clearly, there are beings operating within a larger system, and we — as possessing *human being* — are another kind of being which falls into that relationship of individuals coming together under a larger, overarching happening. And although it could be said that Vim activates these happenings on both individual and macro levels, there is some property that organizes and directs that Vim so that it might operate in the first place, not to mention operate in an efficient manner. This is all to say that Vim is not the only component that makes up Verity. As we have mentioned previously but can now more clearly define: Verity is the thing itself and the sum total of the whole of the individual moments within that thing, as well as those individual movements which comprise its whole. If Verity were a play, the play, of course, would have a stage and a setting — all of which produce action (Vim). But there would also be actors who would read from a script and produce and relay that action to an audience. After all, a real play must be witnessed by an audience — otherwise, it is merely a rehearsal for something more real and of greater consequence. So, what produces the script? Who acts? And who witnesses? Also, what directs the action and who are the actors themselves?

Although Vim and Verity are reality, *in order for anything to be, such a thing must be perceived.*

So, what is it that allows reality to exist?

CONSCIOUSNESS ALLOWS FOR
BEING & PHENOMENA

As it is said about Verity: Vim is all around, constantly working with itself, in itself. Vim is as tangible as it is surreptitious. Both Vim and Verity can be said to have a definite location, yet, at the same time, they are difficult to pin down. To the conceptualized mind, Verity and Vim are tricky to define — much less comprehend.

However, Vim and Verity are only two thirds of the whole. There is another, completely intricate component of their existence: Consciousness. While Vim and Verity are the centralized components of both Being and the events which take place within it, something must exist in congress with Being and phenomena that puts them into play; and that "something" is Consciousness itself.

Nothing can exist without Consciousness. It is, in fact, an extraordinarily simple notion that *a thing cannot exist without something to perceive it.* To have existence is to be perceived. If nothing perceives a thing, how can it be said that such a thing exists? Even if that existence is imperceptible by a particular consciousness, there is *something* which must acknowledge or interact with that thing in order for it to be — which, is simply to say that there can be no thing without an entity that acknowledges or has some kind of interaction with that thing.

For example, we can easily imagine an undiscovered element or an animal species the scientific community is unaware of; however, the scientific community's ignorance does not mean that such a thing does not exist, as this undiscovered thing nevertheless has a kind of being and interacts with or is acknowledged by other beings it has relationships with. For, if a thing exists there must be something that witnesses or in some way interacts with that existence; and that acknowledgement and or interaction is the very cause and sustainer of that thing's existence and vice versa. In the very same way, the capacity for such a thing to be able to interact with other beings and events is set up by the relationship that particular being enjoys with the ultimate witness, Consciousness. For, the witness brings forth the thing. Through acknowledgment, the thing is given the gift of existence itself. To say that a thing can exist without interacting with or being perceived by anything else or is absurd: again, how can a thing have an existence if it has no interactions with other beings or events, or goes completely unrecognized? And yet, existence itself is a *relationship*. So, it begs the question: what is existence a relationship with? It cannot be other Being alone, for, what, then, is the relationship which allows for Being's existence?

To answer such a puzzle, we might look to the likes of another riddle: the famous Zen koan asks, 'If a tree falls in the woods and there is no one there to hear it, does it make a sound?' Although, to truly get to the heart of our issue we must take it a step further and ask, 'If a universe is created and there is no Consciousness there to perceive it, does it really exist at all?' The question is absurd: how can something exist without perception? Quite simply, it cannot. For, existence is an acknowledgement of thinghood. And if there is nothing there to witness the being or event, how can it be acknowledged that such a being or event exists in the first place? After all, it is the perception itself which identifies and allows for the existence of a given thing. Without something to perceive *of*, there is no possibility of existence itself. Existence and perception are one and the same.

PERCEPTION ACTUALIZES BEING

So, modern science must make a rigorous reevaluation of its postulations and ask, 'If, according to our current theories and observations, at the beginning of the universe there was only matter, how did the universe exist?' Which is to ask, 'What perceived the universe at its inception?' We have the luxury here in our war of dispensing with the dramatic uselessness of the kind of debate that might otherwise ensue and cut directly to the answer: what existed at the "beginning of the universe"[32] was Consciousness itself, just as it continues to exist in the present day. Again, in order to have any given thing there must be something which perceives that thing (even if what perceives the thing is the thing itself). If there was no perception *of*, how could we possibly attempt to describe the qualities of a given thing, or the location of it, or that what we were attempting to describe had any degree of thinghood whatsoever? All of this would be utterly impossible — not to mention nonsensical — given the fact that in order to acknowledge a thing one has to have a perception of that thing in the first place; and this does not at all mean that a human being has to perceive of a thing in order for it to exist, for, one could very easily argue that trees that fall in the woods without anyone around to hear them certainly do still produce sound waves and have an effect on the ground they land on. So, the question becomes, 'Even if the tree that falls in the

---

[32] We will later see how time itself is a completely illusory happening; so, to say that there was a "beginning of the universe" is not at all accurate; however, we need to continue to use these kinds of terms from old language for the time being in order to move beyond them.

woods without anyone around doesn't make an audial sound, what is it that perceives of it falling in the first place?' Again, the answer is that something is clearly keeping a watchful eye on the grand scheme of phenomena. Otherwise, beings and events themselves could not exist.

So, we understand Consciousness to be essential to the interactions of Vim and Verity. In fact, it could be said that Consciousness is produced by the interaction between Vim and Verity and vice versa: Verity is generated through Vim (or vice versa), and the happening produced is codified in a metaphysical state of recognition known to us as Consciousness. Consciousness is the grand scribe: it both records and makes possible all of Vim and Verity's products and interactions. Again, there can be no Being or phenomena without the perception *of* Being or phenomena. *Being and phenomena* (which are both forms of Vim and Verity) *need to be perceived in order to exist. There can be no existence without the perception of a thing existing in the first place.* If nothing at all perceives a being or happening, it is impossible to say that there was a "being" or "happening" at all; for, the "being" or "happening" had no stage on which to perform. Being and phenomena must have an audience of some kind in order to exist or occur in the first place. Otherwise, without anything to relate to it — that is, if the being or happening has no other relation to any thing — it cannot exist.

As we have already demonstrated, a particular being comes out of other particular beings (not to mention Being itself), just as events take place somewhere within the grander scheme of phenomena. All beings and phenomena are built upon other beings and other phenomena. So, we see that it is not necessarily the thing or the isolated happening, but the *relation* that is of primary importance when it comes to Being and phenomena. Of course, a being or happening cannot rely merely on other beings or happenings for its existence, because it would encounter the same problem that those other beings and happenings would likewise need something to perceive them in order to initially exist. Obviously, if there was nothing to perceive of those other beings or happenings — much less their relations — there would be no way for the initial being or happening to come into existence. If nothing is there to perceive a thing or an act, then such a thing or act could not have existed initially. Matter cannot be held in existence merely by other matter alone. Existence *is and must be* consciousness *of* existence. There is no being without a perceiver just as there is no act without the actor; both are Consciousness in its various modalities. And, likewise: Consciousness must be conscious *of* something; otherwise it is conscious of *nothing*, and, being so, is not Consciousness.

In order to understand this very basic yet profound rule of Being and phenomena we need to understand that, much like how we have described the relationship between Vim and Verity, Being and phenomena need an activator. Neither a singular being alone nor the larger form of Being itself can serve as the sole catalyst of phenomena, nor can phenomena be the sole cause of Being: both must be acknowledged by something; this is the very definition of existence — that which *is*. Of course, what *is* must be given a life, and, as we have shown, nothing can exist in the vacuum of isolation: all things contain all other things. And the container of all those things is Consciousness itself.

Consciousness is the enabler of action. It is the goldilocks zone and the tar pit of Being: all things are both allowed to act and are at the same time fossilized within Consciousness. Again, without something to perceive *of* a happening, no happening can take place; to say otherwise is oxymoronic. If one *was* to try and argue that a thing happened outside the realm of Consciousness or without a conscious activator, one would be arguing that such a thing happened which could at no time be perceived, felt, or said to have effect or relation — which is the absolute equivalent of saying that a thing does not exist. After all, what would one call a thing that has no quality, attribute, relation, or general being, and, furthermore, because of its lack of quality, attribute, relation, or being, does not play out in phenomena? There is truly nothing one *could* call it; for, one cannot define this so-called "thing" by what it is, but only by what it is not. Therefore, such a "thing" has no existence, and, hence, is *nothing*.

For, again, a thing cannot exist unless it is perceived. Perception is *the* necessary element of action — even if that action is no action — that is, even if it is nothing. Even nothing requires Consciousness to distinguish it from that which has existence. Phenomena and Being require Consciousness for animation and actuality. As we shall discover at greater depth further into our war, a thing (even if that thing is what we might think of as "inanimate") must be aware of itself in order to exist; that is to say that even inanimate properties must either be aware of their properties in order to have them in the first place, or there must be something which is aware of their properties that orchestrates the whole relationality which facilitates their Being. Either way, nothing can be without perception (that is, without Consciousness). Even a rock must understand its hardness in order to exist against and interact with that which is soft; therefore, even the unthinking, inanimate rock has a kind of awareness of itself. And this awareness is nothing short of real and actual Consciousness itself. And Consciousness at any level (if, in fact, it can be said to have levels at all) is the vital third element of Vim and Verity. Again, all three parts might be used interchangeably. Vim and Verity could not be without an awareness of themselves, but their interaction produces Consciousness as much as the mere state of Consciousness allows for Vim and Verity to be. Therefore, when we speak of one, we speak of all three.

THE NEW TRINITY: VIM, VERITY, AND CONSCIOUSNESS[33]

Going further, although we have thus far only begun to rally against the mores and norms of both the past and present (though, to be clear, our defamation of these mores has not yet begun in earnest), we may, in this instance, be able to blaze ahead more quickly by using an old analogy so that we can better understand our future direction: the relationship between Verity, Consciousness, and Vim might be best understood as one similar to the Christian tradition's notion of the Father, Son, and the Holy Spirit. In this analogy, Verity acts as the

---

[33] To fully understand the following, we will have to delve into a slew of Christian terminology to prove our points. However, it should be noted that although the dialect of our veritable philosophy is quite a bit different than the language used by Christianity, at this time we are attempting to prove a similar point as Christian apologists, albeit with several major departures. Here, again, it suits one to keep in mind that fighting language with similar language is the linguistic equivalent of fighting fire with fire.

Father, Consciousness as the Son, and Vim as Holy Spirit. However, before we go into it we must make clear that, unlike Verity and Vim — which are, for lack of a better term, new ideas to our minds — the word "consciousness" is something we generally all have an idea about. However, like everything else in our war, that familiarity must be deconstructed and redefined if we are to aptly use it to our advantage going forward. For, here we must see that consciousness is carried out, at least in part, by ourselves as individuals. Although the level of our consciousness is up for debate, we, as human beings, *are* in fact conscious; this is an extremely important fact going forward: we possess within us and are intimately aware of a key component of the makeup of reality (the interplay between Vim and Verity) itself. In fact, we might go so far as to argue that Consciousness is *the* key component. And while we can contemplate our varying degrees of our awareness and interactions about and with Vim and Verity, that we are at least partially conscious can be easily seen by all. Again, the importance of this cannot be understated: that we are conscious means that we are the torchbearers of a great and vital component of the universe and reality (Verity) itself. Within the microcosm of our beings the larger cosmic force which upholds the rest of creation is radically present. For, within us there is Consciousness, and Consciousness is that which is responsible for all Being and action; again, there can be nothing without it.

But the most important thing for us to comprehend here is that *we* as individuals are the key components in Verity's ultimate happening. Unlike the Christian trinitarian notion of an all-powerful father, the medium of a holy spirit, and a human embodiment of these two interplays of "God" on earth in Jesus Christ, what Verity allows for is the transformation of the figure of Christ squarely into our own beings. That is to say that if the power of the Christian trinity is in the father, son, and holy spirit, the power of the veritable trinity is in Verity, Vim, and one's own self. For, Being comes out of Consciousness and not the their way around — as much of modern science (led by the blind eyes of conceptualization, of course) would claim. There is great responsibility in this: as conscious beings we are the shepherds of Verity just as much as Verity is of us; the relationship is precisely equal: one creates the other. As human beings alive within Verity, we enjoy the dialectical experience of being both fully human and at the same time fully divine.

Through the power of Consciousness we see that we, as individuals, bring about and sustain Vim and Verity, just as Consciousness sustains all things — both physical and metaphysical. It is our own conscious beings that invoke Vim and Verity and all the physiological and metaphysical things that go along with it.[34] The empowering thing about Vim and Verity, however, is that, unlike the Christian trinity, it is the individual human being who is the third most intricate prong of the holy triangle. Our movement puts us on equal footing with the godheads of the old religions; and that is its power. Of course, at the apex of many of the old religions, the "God"

---

[34] There is another philosophical / scientific realm of thought that has gained a quasi-commercial popularity here in the early part of the 21st century called "Bio-centrism" which similarly states that instead of the physical world creating life, life creates the physical world. Although the parallels here are obvious, as we shall see, Biocentrism and our philosophy of Vim, Verity, & Consciousness took different paths — and, in fact, are out to accomplish different missions. However, both seem to arrive at a similar conclusion.

described is often both physically and emotionally aloof and almost always difficult to understand in its actions and reasoning. But the beauty of Christ is that he transcends both God the Father and humanity by becoming both fully "God" and fully human at the same time. However, our veritable philosophy takes this transcendence a step further and puts this figure of Christ squarely within *each of us*. It is no longer the case that 'the almighty' has bestowed itself into a singular individual, but rather that the divine has distributed itself into all of humankind equally. That is to say that in our veritable philosophy, here, within our war, we – as conscious human beings – are the equivalents of the Christ figure in Christianity. And while some Christians might see this statement as blasphemy, the intent is wholly the opposite: we only mean to say that there exists an ultimacy within each of us; whether or not one believes it to be bestowed upon us through Christ or Consciousness itself is a matter of linguistic gymnastics: both have the same meaning and it is not our purpose here to attempt to offend anyone's beliefs, or, much more importantly, anyone's faith.[35]

However, that being said, the burden of this notion of divine responsibility is taken off of a singular savior and laid heavily upon *us*: it binds us to the cosmic forces and holds us solely culpable for their proper implementations; which is to say that we as individuals hold the grand powers of the universe

---

[35] However, in subsequent chapters we will launch an entire assault on the belief system itself. Yet, as we shall see even further on in our war, one's faith is paramount to victory in this or any other battle, and, therefore, it must be kept intact by any means necessary. But our mission here is as performative as anything: we need to evoke a certain awareness about the state of things, and using a new language in order to do so is the surest way to accomplishing this task. The details, however, are of little importance: that is, whether one believes in Christ or in Verity, both are simply the scenery which sets the stage that points to the larger happening beyond them.

itself within our very beings and, given this to be the case, we are responsible for the proper administration of these powers in whatever forms they may take. In our philosophy of Verity, the savior we seek out exists within us. And yet, at the same time, Verity is an omnipresent being whose state we all eventually default into. So, while we have the responsibility of salvation within us, we also have the security of Verity all around us. And while Verity escapes the exacting definitions associated with particular things, it is conscious, and, thus, personable. And it is this personability that sets up the humanity within each of us — a humanity which is similarly projected back out into the world in a double reflection. We give rise to Verity just as Verity gives rise to us; and both happen under the firmament of Consciousness.

VERITY MUST BE KNOWN & EXPERIENCED

If, in Christianity, we have an unplaceable god whose being we cannot fully understand (much less see), in Vim and Verity we not only have a direct relation *to* them given our mutual bond through Consciousness, but we have a real and substantial influence *on* them as well. Verity, as both a being and phenomenon, removes the need for an intermediary; or, more accurately, the intermediary between Verity and Consciousness is what we perceive of as the individual self, and this perceptibly individual self can communicate directly with Verity through that mutually shared state of Consciousness. Again, it is Consciousness that activates all things — including Verity. In fact, reality demands that it be known and experienced — otherwise it would not be reality! Therefore, there is no way around the fact that all things are infused with Verity, and Verity (unlike the traditional notion of a biblical or esoteric "God") cannot be denied, being that it *is* what *is*. Of course, reality can only be known through the consciousness it employees, and its conscious agents are found in all manners of Being and phenomena.

CONCEPTS HAVE ISOLATED VERITY

Reality cannot escape itself any more than we can escape it; and, through our own individualized consciousness, what we think of as "ourselves" and Verity cannot be separated. Whereas conceptualization's dangerous power and ever-persistent threat is that through its implementation we *can* escape from Verity by turning our focus away from it and creating a new kind of consciousness built on precepts and fabricated conditionality. However, the tricky thing with Verity is its malleability. In fact, being that whatever *is* is Verity (even if what "is" is ultimately proven to have an element of illusion), concepts, too, are also components of Verity.

Because concepts *are*, they are also forms of Verity; that is, concepts, too, have existence and are real, and that existence makes them veritable. Of course, there is no degree to Verity: a thing is either real or it is not. However, and, again, the difficulty with concepts and illusions is that they too have their own kind of existences; however, their existences are predicated on foundations that begin to break down as their layers are peeled away. So, while a certain veritable thing cannot be any less veritable than another, if such a thing is truly veritable it has a direct linkage back to all other Verity, whereas concepts eventually begin to dry out and come up against that which is ultimately untrue and unverifiable. One might say that concepts are veritable in isolation only, but begin to lose their veritability when absorbed by the totality of Verity. Whereas, something that was truly veritable would always continue to be, because it is, of course, real.

For example, an oasis in the desert containing veritable trees and water is contingent on *the whole of existence in order to be*: whereas, the mirage of an oasis has a reality as an illusion, but, as an illusion, it is dependent upon *a particular consciousness or perception in order to be*. If the particular consciousness propagating the illusion changed or ceased, the illusion would vanish along with it: whereas, the veritable oasis could not be snuffed out by a particular consciousness or perception, being that it is supported by the whole of Verity itself.

THE ILLUSORY STATE OF CONCEPTS

Another example (and one we will explore quite a bit further in our direct battle with it) is language: language is a mere combination of audible sounds or written or signaled characters that come together in a certain way to form a communication of some kind or another. However, the word "tree", even though it has a degree of reality to it, is not a tree itself but only a representation of the actual thing which exists within phenomena that we label as a tree. Though, outside of our mind's own understanding of what the word "tree" represents, there is no reality attached to the word other than the one we conjure up — and that conjuring is only brought about through the other ideas and relations we hold within our mind.

The word has no reality outside of the reality we give to it through other ideas; *that is what a concept is: it is something which has no actuality outside of our own minds.* However, the thing about concepts is that they often operate as if they had sufficiently filled the mysterious gaps of knowledge we have about a given thing; that is to say that concepts act as though they were an absolute veritable happening or being. Whereas something that is truly veritable has linkage back to that which has an independent existence outside of our mind's own conjurings. Concepts lose validity and credulity the further and further back they are peeled, whereas something veritable is simply there whether or not one is conscious of it.

Therefore, to clarify: Verity is anything that is real. Of course, philosophers will debate about what "reality" is and is not, and, furthermore, they will debate about epistemology and how we are able to discern knowledge altogether. Fortunately, we do not have those difficulties: for, with Verity, all things have some dimension of reality within them. Again, anything that *is* must be conceived *by* something; therefore, Being and Consciousness are inextricably intertwined. And given that Consciousness and Being have this relationship to one another, whatever is perceived has a degree of Verity within it — even concepts, or even things that exist solely within one's imagination. Concepts have a reality in the minds which perceive them, but if those minds were to change or cease to be, those thoughts and ways of life dictated by those concepts would similarly perish. So, concepts do have a certain reality, and, in fact, humanity's power lies in our capacity to turn our ideas into realities — which is to say that we are capable of creating veritable states (both physical and nonphysical) out of our metaphysical minds; this kind of gift was one previously reserved only for the gods, and yet, we have it in abundance.

REMOVAL OF THE PRIME MOVER

Being and phenomena have veritable existences because they are directly linked to Consciousness. The question is, however, on what grounds do these veritable beings and events play out? That is, exactly what or whose consciousness perceives the thing when it exists or occurs?

It has previously been said by other philosophers and theologians that "God" is the "ground of Being" — which makes "God" the playing field from which Being springs forth. In Verity, however, no such "God" is needed. Being and Consciousness rely on one another for their existences; thus, there is no "God" that brings things into or out of existence or is the prime mover or alpha: Being, events, and Consciousness all operate on equal ground. Furthermore, no deity or biological thing must be present to witness the event's occurrence, as Verity itself is *also* Consciousness itself. That which is veritable is conscious, and that which is conscious is veritable. So, even things we think of as unconscious or inanimate have a direct correlation to Consciousness.

INDIVIDUAL BEINGS & EVENTS ARE MERE FINGERS ON THE HAND OF CONSCIOUSNESS

Where we get into a great amount of difficulty, however, is not so much that we utilize conceptualization as a tool, but more so that we treat concepts as concretized facts that have realities outside of our mental constructs. And when concepts are treated as realities, the world is experienced at a degree removed from Verity. Though, ironically, Verity itself is often wholly unmysterious and altogether easily accessed. In fact, the human consciousness's greatest difficulty with Verity might well be that it is so easily accessed that its presence is almost always overlooked. And while conceptualization is a tool we can use to interact with and further comprehend Verity through, it must be used like any other tool and put down after its work is completed. For, a consciousness which relies too heavily on conceptualization is not nimble, active, agile, and, most importantly, aware.

Of course, awareness is the entire objective of Consciousness. And for Verity to exist, Consciousness must play a part. Therefore, Verity is both given a life and affirms itself through Consciousness. For, Verity cannot be apart from Consciousness; because, as we have stated, Verity and Consciousness serve to compose and sustain one another. When, kenotically, Verity empties itself into Being it is not so much that multiple beings are created, but it is more accurate to say that Verity creates various forms of itself that interact with one another. And the interaction of Verity with Verity creates deeper and deeper states of awareness. Even though these various beings may have different accesses to Consciousness — which, to an outside observer may make it appear as though those various forms are conscious beings with different minds and experiences — the experiences they have and the consciousness they cultivate are still partaking in the larger happenings of both Being and Consciousness and, at their cores, cannot be said to ultimately be two different things. More accurately, they are equivalent to various fingers on the same hand: one may be of different length or at a different position, but both are of the same hand, and, what's more, the same body.

VERITY'S NATURAL COURSE

One of the innumerable dangers of conceptualization is that it has the ability to turn a particular conscious individual away from that which is veritable and create within that consciousness the false idol of idealism. Clearly, concepts alter Verity's natural relationship with a particular consciousnesses; however, because it gives gravitas to all things, Verity simply conforms even to the constructs of concepts themselves and grants them their own veritability. So, again, this is the danger of conceptualization: if we do not dethrone it, then, before long, we become lost in the self-created fog of our own skewed "reality". And this new, skewed reality is, of course, entirely divergent from Verity's original trajectory.

Now, many will ask what Verity's original or natural course is, or if we can even know it. Still other, more clever epistemological antagonists will point out that given how expansive concepts' invasion of our minds has become, how could we possibly know what is a veritable being or experience and what is not? However, the answers — like all things within Verity — are simple: Verity always finds its natural course, and if ever it were to be taken astray, being true to itself, it will always eventually revert to what it actually *is*. After all, it would be ontologically impossible for true reality to permanently be led apart from itself; that is, something truly and originally veritable could not be permanently sustained by a concept, otherwise it would not be truly or originally veritable: the being or event would revert back to its originality once the mental constructions propping it up were no longer in play. Again, Verity is itself and all other things within Consciousness, so while it can be consciously led by various degrees or levels of consciousness — including concepts — it can never be led wholly asunder.

A NEW ACTION

Here we need to take the time to explore the possibility that — given that all Being and phenomena are merely components of Verity, and thus, in their true essence, various components of Consciousness itself — there is an entirely different way we might be able to consciously act. Currently, many of the actions employed by human beings are motivated by a sense of our isolated individuality; that is to say that we often act as though we are subjective beings alive within and against a greater totality of which we are both a part of and removed from at the same time. However, if we are able to understand that what we perceive of as individualized beings are more like the above mentioned "fingers on the hand of Consciousness" then we might be able to both physically and metaphysically connect to one another in ways our current mental conditioning prohibits us from doing. This is not to disregard the obvious fact that human beings are individuals whom exist within the realm of Being. However, our individuality is linked through the proverbial Ariadne's thread of Consciousness. As beings in the universe, we are less like separate animal species and far more akin to a grove of trees all sharing the same root system of Consciousness.

Yet, one might argue that, through conceptualization, the grand happening of Consciousness now drunkenly perceives itself as fragmented individuality. However, even if this was the case, one might just as easily argue that there is a greater potential for Consciousness to sustain itself if it disseminated into a myriad of beings much in the way a plant disperses many seeds in the hopes that one takes root and grows. In fact, by dispensing Consciousness into a multitude of beings, Verity gains the capacity to be itself while at the same time existing as wholly other than itself. And if we understand it to be the case that we as human beings are not only individuals that happen to be conscious, but that we are, at the same time, Consciousness that has manifested itself into various individualities, then our interconnectedness becomes as evident as it is potentially effectual because of this new perception. After all, we invoke and interact with our own consciousness and the consciousness of other beings simply by engaging with phenomena; so, our mere existence furthers both our own consciousness and the grander understanding of Consciousness as a whole.

To carry the point further, given that Consciousness expands and understands itself all the more through its own interactions with itself, Verity would be wise to create its own polarity so that it might comprehend itself through the lens of its opposition. That is to say that it is wholly conceivable that Verity would need conceptualization to understand itself to its fullest, and thus, reaffirm itself. So, it is entirely possible that Verity uses conceptualization to become more conscious of itself. In this way, just as with all of its many other implements, Consciousness goes through a process and evolves. And it seeks out this evolution through whatever means it has at its disposal. Although, the danger of using conceptualization to further Consciousness's own evolution is that, like a drug, if conceptualization is utilized too frequently then Consciousness risks inebriation and the attached hazards of no longer being able to operate independently of conception (at least, for a time).

So, although it may seem to run counter to nearly all of what we have said about it up to this point, conceptualization — as a tool — can be extraordinarily useful! However, where its usefulness becomes a detriment to the consciousness which implements it is in conceptualization's inability to relinquish itself. For, conceptualization needs other concepts to keep itself alive; therefore, concepts must continue to breed in order to survive, whereas Verity need not do anything at all in order to ensure its viability.

BEING IS THE CONTENT OF CONSCIOUSNESS: CONSCIOUSNESS IS THE ACTIVATOR OF BEING

Vim is the activator of Verity: it is the force behind all things — the animator of all realities. Vim apprehends itself through its own acts, and, doing so, might be described as conscious; that is to say that Vim's actions often create or define a relationship between various entities or play a part in the trajectory of a larger action which sets up further relations. And through those relations there is an order which is set up within the scope of Verity itself. So, Vim is the guiding principle behind the happening. And once certain relations are defined there are various interplays of Vim that exist between those entities that are intentional and purposeful in their own right.

For example, the relationship between a mountain and the stream produces a very particular, yet intentional kind of interaction between the two entities: the stream exists on the mountain because the mountain's slope and height allows for the stream to form; and the stream's formation will then provide nourishment for vegetation on the mountain, which, in turn, helps to stabilize the earth that the mountain is made up of, thus, helping to keep the mountain from eroding. In another example, a hydrogen and oxygen molecule existing as independent elements join in a very particular way to produce water. And while we can say that these kinds of acts between entities are not intentional in the way a person might, for example, exercise with the intent of maintaining a healthy lifestyle, there is no doubt that the acts between inanimate beings *do* produce happenings that are so effective in their interplay that it is difficult to say that the acts are in themselves arbitrary.

Although, to say that Vim is "conscious" in the ways that a human being or an animal with a nervous system is conscious may not be entirely accurate given that beings with a nervous system tend to gain conscious experiences through the results of the sensory perceptions their nervous systems afford them. Traditionally, what we have come to understand a "conscious organism" to be is more in sync with the biological being that gains an experience through the utilization of its senses and then relays those experiences to the brain, thus forming what we refer to as a 'conscious experience or interpretation'. And while our understanding of 'conscious beings' may already be defined, that understanding only speaks to a fragment of the grand happening of Consciousness itself. For, Consciousness is a happening that extends well beyond a biological byproduct; for, again, Consciousness is a part of Being itself.

Consciousness is an awareness *of*. So, for Consciousness to occur, it must have an object to direct itself towards — which is to say that it cannot exist without something which gives it its awareness. Again, in biological beings it is the nervous system which allows for a conscious experience. Consciousness is an action in biological beings: it is something that happens *to* that being given the proper firing of the nervous system. However, to say that consciousness is merely something that is a product of biology shortchanges the grander 'thinghood' of Consciousness.[36] For, Consciousness is not only something gained through biology: it is tapped into by all of Being's manifestations. Consciousness and Being are, in fact, two renderings of a singular movement. After all, Consciousness must be aware *of* something. And Being must be recognized *by* something in order to *be*. Consciousness must have content. Being must have acknowledgement. Being is the content of Consciousness. And Consciousness is the sustainer of Being.

VERITY CONSCIOUSLY INTERACTS WITH ITSELF, THUS CREATING OTHER MODES OF BEING & CONSCIOUSNESS

Vim both manifests into and also activates Being. Through this transmutation, the singular being becomes a part of the larger whole of Verity. Verity, on a macro level, is the amalgamate of all the manifests of Vim and its byproduct, Being. All the interactions of Verity with itself come to create modes of Being,

---

[36] Wherever "Consciousness" is capitalized we mean for it to symbolize this grander happening or "thinghood" of Consciousness.

which, through those interactions, then go on to further define other modes of Being and interaction. Through this process of Being interacting with and relating to other Being, an awareness is created about those beings and their interactions which then goes on to create further acts, other modes, and more kinds of Being. This entire process takes a joint awareness of the mode, action, and being, which — although it might not be so readily identified as the brand of consciousness we have come to understand — is, in fact, an awareness, nevertheless. For, there could be no act in the first place without Consciousness playing a central role.

BECAUSE CONSCIOUSNESS IS A VITAL COMPONENT, ACTION & BEING ARE NOT ARBITRARY

No action is wholly random: all things within time have a predecessor, and the singular action or being derives itself from a web of other actions, modalities, and beings which have their own genesis in similar forces and fashions. That is to say that no act or being within time can exist in isolation, so, the mere fact that a thing is birthed means that it was produced through other acts or forces which came together to craft it. Because, even that which might be regarded as an inanimate force still holds a particular relation to all the other forces and beings it comes up against; and those other forces or modes of Being or actions interact with one another and set up particular relations which define and mold those forces or beings. So, in the interaction itself there is a kind of ongoing awareness that is continually being set up and defined between the various forces or beings. That awareness — although we do not traditionally identify it as such — is Consciousness in action. However, this brand of consciousness is not taking place within a biological entity, but rather between two "inanimate" forces or beings.

For example, a rock understands that it is a rock not because it has a mind akin to the kind a biological entity possesses, but it understands itself to be a rock by what composes it and by what it stands against. A rock does not mistake itself to be a tree or a giraffe, but, due to both its own composition and the relationality it enjoys with all other forms of existence, is wholly aware of its being, and, by extension, its general role and purpose. (That is to say that a rock is simply a rock and its purpose is fulfilled by its very being.) The relationality of the rock to other forms of Verity then sets up further relations within phenomena, and Being's various components and relations come to understand itself all the more through its own double reflection. Again, it is not so much that the rock enjoys the kind of consciousness that living entities experience, but its existence alone is a part of all other existence, and is, therefore, ensconced within Being and Consciousness as a whole; this being the case, at the same time one cannot accurately say that the rock is devoid of, at least, a certain brand of awareness — even if that awareness is merely underwritten by Consciousness as a grand form.

So, Consciousness is both a byproduct of Vim's activities and at the same time an essential component to Verity itself; for, again, whatever has a veritable existence also exists within the field of the grander form and happening of Consciousness. In this manner, it would be correct to say that Consciousness operates both as a field and as the product produced by the field itself. For, when various forms of Being are birthed and become veritable entities they interact with one another and, through those interactions, Consciousness becomes further and further aware of itself. And while different conscious perceptions may have various recognitions of a veritable happening, it is only through those many conscious outlooks that Being can further evolve.

THE BEING OF VIM & VERITY

At the risk of belaboring the point we must continue to define our terms. (When painting on a philosophical canvas one must often use the brightest of imaginable colors and then reuse them over and over until the eyes of the beholders begin to bleed.) And while Verity, Vim, and Consciousness might be difficult to grasp at times due to their seemingly abstract natures, it is of paramount importance that we recognize them fully if we are to be successful in our crusade against the enemy of conceptualization.

Verity is reality. It is that which *is*. It is both the many forms of Being and the formless place which, through Vim, births those forms. It is the thing and the nothing between things. Anything that *is* — even nothing — is Verity. Old Language would define Verity as the "godhead". Going further with such terminology, it is the "logos", the *thing*. All reality is Verity and vice versa.

Vim is Verity's Power. Vim is a formless force that creates and destroys Verity. (Although, it, too, is also Verity because it is a reality.) However, Vim is a power that has no location or exacting duty or relation — though, it is the cause and diffuser of all relations. Vim is the ineffable thing which activates life and gives Consciousness a space in which to operate, thereby bringing Verity forth and presenting it to itself, thus, causing and sustaining it.

THE BEING OF CONSCIOUSNESS

Through this interplay of Vim and Verity, Consciousness is simultaneously created; and yet, Consciousness must be present for there to be any action of Vim in the first place; so, to state that Consciousness comes out of Vim and Verity's interactions is merely a misunderstanding of the notion of time (which we will address in a later battle). In the meanwhile, suffice it to say that Consciousness is something not so much created as it is awakened by Vim. Through Vim's operations Verity is created, reality formed, and thus, observed through Consciousness in Consciousness's grand and lesser forms alike. This so-called "grand form of Consciousness" is the metaphysical space which operates in conjunction with Vim and Verity: it is the place from which individual entities derive their own unique consciousnesses and various perspectives. It is commonly referred to as the "collective consciousness", or the "universal mind". The relationship between the grand form of Consciousness and the individual being that possesses consciousness operates in much the same way that a television or a computer operates with its signal: there is a seemingly invisible beacon in the air that is picked up on when an individual entity is properly attuned. Clearly, Consciousness is substantial, cosmic matter, and is as much a part of the make-up of the universe as any other element.

However, for our purposes it may best suit us to understand the grand form of Consciousness as the place which, like

Vim's relation to Verity, makes individualized consciousness a possibility while simultaneously acting as a bank in which those conscious experiences are deposited. And, of course, as we have already demonstrated, Consciousness is not necessarily restricted to beings with nervous systems, but is extended to all veritably existing entities which, through their mere veritibility, serve to influence and inform all Being, phenomena, and thus, Consciousness. Merely because things act as they do, we can understand them to be conscious. *A thing's Being is its awareness.* For, again, Being and Consciousness are one and the same. That a thing *is* demonstrates its undeniable fact that is it aware of its own selfhood. And this simplistic awareness of selfhood is a conscious act. A thing's existence is a confession of its realized state and the relations it holds to all other things within the phenomenological field.[37]

TIME & CONSCIOUSNESS

Another foolproof indicator of the grand form of Consciousness at work is the presence of time. Time is the memory of the universe. And the existence of a memory is an obvious product of Consciousness. That time is implicit in the cosmological fabric points to the irrefutable fact that Consciousness is the real element at play, whereas time is merely its visible form. Time

---

[37] "Phenomena", as classically defined within the field of philosophy, is any act or being that is consciously observed. Of course, as we are noting here, exactly *how* an individual consciousness is able to observe is determined by its capacity — a capacity which is determined by its structure, which, in kind, is determined by its relationships to concepts and reality. In our slightly nuanced understanding, the word "phenomena", as used throughout our work, is the interfacing of action, Being, Vim, Verity, and Consciousness.

allows for various forms of Being and events to evolve and play out against one another. Time also etches these interactions into its own fabric and, piece by piece, relays those interactions to other forms and events so that they too might observe and interact with each other in their own ways, thus creating time; for, it is not so much that events play out within time, but more so that events play out and *create* time. Time and events are one and the same: there can be no time without events occurring, just as events cannot unfold apart from time.[38]

So, time is the field within which evolution occurs. Time allows for process. And process occurs when various forms come up against one another. These forms come to create a happening, and this happening creates more time, continuing the cycle. Therefore, time helps bring things into a presence. And in this presence, the things gain a certain awareness of both themselves and of the various relations they help to compose. Again, an individual thing's being is its awareness of its own self, so, time is merely the marker by which we can identify all the various stations within the general form of Being; that is, at a given time one is able to describe a particular thing and those various relations to it. So, time is a marker we can look to and gain a certain understanding about things as they are.

Of course, events are continually playing out, thus, creating time. So, time is the product of events unfolding, but it is also the scribe of all phenomena. Time records events as they occur. This record is then passed onto the next moment, which also takes a cosmic snapshot of the universe and replicates the process

---

[38] This happening is likely more a product of our consciousness and not so much the product of time. For, events could occur instantly and outside of time given the proper conscious structure.

repeatedly. Of course, to record anything is to have a memory of that happening, and memory is the recall of prior events. Prior events come to inform present events, which, of course, then influence future occurrences. So, time affords the opportunity for beings and events to communicate with one another, connecting all with all in its ever-persistent unfolding of the present. And within that unfolding of time it is the present that ultimately bridges all gulfs between all things. Yet, strangely enough, all things operate solely *in* the present, which obscures the past and future into something of a smoky mirage. Of course, there is nothing in the realm of phenomena that is not connected by the present. Therefore, the present puts all things in touch, and in this way becomes the language of Consciousness. (Though, as we shall see, language is an imperfect tool to say the least.) Time, however, is a system (which is another enemy of Verity that will be heavily dealt with later on), and, being so, has a limited capacity for true and unfettered interaction with what *is*.

Given the fact that the academic disciplines are fueled entirely by an evolved conceptualization, time is almost uniformity misunderstood across modern academia. These misunderstandings begin with the notion that time is an inherent structure of the cosmos and that physical space and time are bonded together into a singular happening called "spacetime".[39] However, what is almost universally overlooked is the fact that without Consciousness, neither time, space, nor Being itself would be possible; for, again, there can be no thing without something to observe the thing. Nothing can be

---

[39] Spacetime is a four-dimensional structure that is believed to be the essential makeup of the universe itself: it involves three dimensions of direction and one direction of time all inextricably interwoven together.

said to exist without the observation of its existence;[40] to say otherwise is purely absurd.

And although it is a significant component, time is merely just another product within Consciousness's vast inventory. For, as with Being and events (and all other forms of Verity), time has no location without something to recognize and observe it. Time is only a tool that Consciousness implements when perceiving events. That is, when events play out, they are observed by Consciousness, and this observation of the events unfolding is a kind of record-keeping that gives rise to the process we refer to as time.

Ironically, however, although it may seem as though it is a facet of the dimensionality of our universe, time is arguably the greatest conception of all. For time requires Consciousness to be constructed in a very particular and systematic way: time follows precise rules and paths, adhering to all kinds of restraints and limitations depending on exactly what it is that is observing it.[41] In this way, time is governed by the kind of consciousness

---

[40] Here one might argue that a thing can be inferred to exist without actually observing its existence. For thousands of years the atom was inferred to have an existence, and when the modern microscope was invented the existence of the atom was observed, and thus, empirically confirmed. However, this is not what is meant when it is said that "Nothing can be said to exist without the observation of its existence". For, clearly, *something* observed the atom to exist before our human consciousnesses were able to confirm it. So, suffice it to say that a thing does not need human verification in order to have existence, but it must be observed by *something* — even if that observation takes place in its relationality to other modes of Being, events, or even its own self.

[41] Here is where the theory of relativity showed that its poetic prowess far out-powered its scientific one: relativity demonstrated that the way time was experienced depended on the observer. In this way, time — much like everything else — is a product of its relationality. One observer will experience time in a completely different manner than another observer — which further demonstrates that time is a mere component of Consciousness itself.

possessed by the observer. And in a consciousness dominated by concepts, time becomes an operation that opposes the unbounded, limitless powers of Vim. Therefore, time has become the imprisonment of the conceptualized mind; so, to free oneself of time is to do away with one of concept's most dominating forces. However, here we must ask ourselves if it is possible to cast time away as if it were a dirty garment. Given our current structures and understanding of science, such a feat seems impossible. Yet, we must again remember that time is a product of the relation a consciousness has with Verity. And one's conscious experience is determined by the structure of one's consciousness — meaning that, if we were to change the structure of our consciousness, the structure of time, like all of conception's tools, would likewise change along with it. Such a change *is* possible. The question is, are we ready for it?

THE STRUCTURE OF TIME

Although we shall deal with the subject of time in its due course, we can presently use time as an ally for our own purposes of presenting it as irrefutable evidence of the grand form of Consciousness: again, without something to observe and structure it, time could not exist in the first place.

Time is the conscious record of Being and happening in the universe. If a thing is purported to have a past, the indictment is that such a thing had a relationality with all other beings and events in existence in that past, meaning that this thing's existence was observed and in some way influenced by the relationality it had to all the other things which existed in the past and continue to exist presently. Again, a thing is granted its existence by that which opposes it: a rock is a rock by standing against a tree or the ocean and all other Being; by standing against all creation, creation itself is acknowledging and allowing for the presence of the rock. Of course, the trick of time is that it can only be observed through the present (which is perfectly logical once we realize that time is merely a product of Consciousness itself); so, to attempt to say anything about the past has to be done through the lens of the present. However, if a thing *is* observed to have had a past, its past existence implies that there was something to have likewise observed it at that time (in the past); for, if it were not observed or not related to all other Being it would not have had an existence in the first place.

But time is the structure by which Consciousness relates to the conceptualized mind. Again, however, in Verity (and or reality) there is no such thing that can be pointed to and called "time", as Verity stands in pure existence without the need for a supporting agency aside from its activator in Vim. Yet, time is a valuable tool of communication between Verity and the conceptualized consciousness: it allows for form to present itself in a way that a conceptualized mind can study and grasp. Time implies process and evolution. The conceptualized consciousness needs evolution in order to re-obtain a veritable state — which is the goal of any individualized consciousness that finds itself separated from Verity. And time is the crutch by which conception grapples with Being and events. Because, the conceptualized mind can only deal with any particular being in pieces: to realize the whole of any given thing at once must be done within a field completely independent from the constraints of time, and a conceptualized mind is incapable of this timeless, holistic approach, much less a brand of unfettered comprehension that puts the individualized consciousness directly in touch with what is being observed without the buffer or barrier of time.

However, that things play out within the process of evolution means that they exist in the field of time — which indicates that whatever that thing is has been observed by some kind of consciousness or a relationality to other beings and events. If we were speaking in purely scientific terms, we would say that Thing Z has a history based on its many relations to Things A —Y. That Thing Z has Being means that it has a "past", and that past is recorded by and imprinted in time, which means that it has had an impact, influence, and relationality to all other Being. This relationality gives the thing its own being — its thinghood — but it also gives it a place within an antiquity that etches itself in the impressions of all beings and events that seemingly follow it. For, the past composes the present, and the present lays the foundation for the future. However, the past, present, and future are only matters of perspective, and perspective is the luxury of the beholder. If a consciousness is properly attuned to Verity, what that consciousness is capable of beholding is accomplished without the hindering obstructions of time; if a consciousness is not attuned, however, time will always be a factor. (Though it should be recognized that if time *is* an ally of any given thing it seldom holds on to that fidelity for long.)

THE IMPOTENCE OF SCIENCE IN RELATIONSHIP TO TIME

The scientific elements which often dominate these kinds of dialogues amongst topics of this nature would have us focus on the physicalities of the structures within Being. Science centers itself on the empirical aspects of Verity that can be obtained through sensory perception. However, science has nothing to say about Vim; it has nothing to say about the force behind the observable action, and yet it is that force which is of supreme importance to our comprehension of the totality. After all, we should not think to understand a human being by one's skin alone (not that this viewpoint hasn't been attempted in the past). And yet, it is this very approach that we take when deciphering the nature of the universe: we put all our stock into the physicalities and little if any into the *intent* or the *trajectory* of a given thing. For, science can only observe the repetition of the pattern. Simply put, science is the observation of repetition. And although science can make any number of inferences about the intentions of the things it observes, it is not necessarily in the business of giving reasons for *why* things do what they do (nor could it ever, to any adequate degree).

And yet, any veritable form is much more than the physical shell observable through scientific lenses. As we have noted, there is something that drives all form and gives it its power and essence: this source is Vim. Where Verity is the thing, Vim is that which flows through the thing and relates it to all other things.[42] And though we place stock into the empirical observations we as human beings make about the phenomenological world, what we think of as reality is actually dictated solely by the capacities granted to us through our sensory perceptions — all of which are unrefined, and, hence, limited.

---

[42] Here, we mean "Things" as both beings and events, respectively.

THE OBSERVER IS THE OBSERVED

However, when an individual consciousness is able to observe a thing without preconception, that consciousness literally merges with that thing it observes and the distinction between the observer and that which is observed melts away. For, again, Consciousness and Being are two sides of the same event, and without concepts impeding the observation of a happening, the observer herself vanishes and becomes a mere vestige for Consciousness to simply flow through and pay attention to the object of its focus. In this pure interaction with a veritable object, the observer is conjoined to the essence of Verity and the two become indistinguishably unified. Such an action is a kind of cooperation between the individual and Verity, and in this allegiance a partnership that has no true delineation between the self and the thing that might otherwise be considered outside the self is formed. And when Consciousness merges in earnest with its content, not only does the distinguishment between the observer and the observed drop away, but time, likewise, becomes nonexistent. For, time is the product of various things at play with one another. However, when things act in a unified movement in and with Verity, there is no separation, and, hence, no thing which then produces time in the way our consciousness currently experiences it given its present form.

BEING WITH: HOW THE STRUCTURE OF CONSCIOUSNESS HELPS SHAPE VERITY ITSELF

Here we need to understand just how intimately related to Verity Consciousness really is. Likewise, human beings — all of whom have varying degrees of access to Consciousness as a structure — are not so much cogs within the great cosmic wheel, but, being a part of Consciousness itself, have true and real influence over the direction of how the grand form of Consciousness operates. As we noted earlier, many have referred to this so-called "grand form of Consciousness" as the "collective consciousness". However, the term "collective conscious" here seems too linguistically far off (not to mention too new-aged and potentially watered down because of it) to demonstrate the ready-to-hand influence an individual can have on Consciousness itself. As we have also already remarked, Consciousness is a larger, independent happening that individuals simply attune to. Yet, much like a user connected to the world wide web, the individual can influence and significantly alter the grander form of Consciousness. This is one of the things that makes the age of the internet so fascinating: the internet operates in the exact same manner as Consciousness itself; in fact, the cyber universe of the world wide web is akin to the physical manifest of the relationship between Consciousness and the individual. When a user on the world wide web uploads content, all the other users connected to the internet then have access to it. And while there are those who are unaware that a certain thing exists on the web, it is nevertheless accessible to every user. Of course, what is uploaded to the web is then often refined, critiqued, commented on, and replicated; the same can be said of the grand form of Consciousness: the conscious acts of one individual will influence the actions and understanding of another, which will influence another, and so on and so forth.

Yet, again, it's worth remembering that the means by which we currently access Consciousness largely depends on conceptualization, and, being so, puts us at varying degrees of odds with Verity; and one of these degrees goes on to structure Consciousness in such a way that it creates the product of time. But true action within Verity has no time, because it is acting *with* the entire structure of reality; it is not acting against or opposed to something — which, again, creates the illusion of process and time. However, this action with and within Verity is highly creative, and within that creativity there *is* a happening, yet, the happening takes place outside of the conventional parameters and restraints forged from linear time as it is "normally" experienced. (Of course, again, what is "normal" is a matter of how a particular consciousness is structured.) When one interacts purely with Verity, something is tapped into that harnesses the creative powers of Vim itself, and in that interaction, there is a joint movement that is neither scripted nor controlled, but, again, is pure happening itself.

This happening has been called many things by old language: many Western traditions call it a "communion with God", but we have shown that the word "God" is archaic to the point of obscurity in the present age; so, to refer to it in this way would mix and confuse two different traditions. A word that is still imprisoned by old language yet is closer to the kind of happening we're attempting to describe would be "meditation". However, meditation is commonly thought of as more of an intentional practice, whereas the kind of happening we speak of can take place through either intention or spontaneity. And though meditation can be done in a variety of different ways on many multitudes of levels, it often has a goal or an aim in mind, whereas the happening we describe most often does not. Yet, the word "meditation" is extremely close to the kind of experience we speak of, though, it is imperfect — with its largest flaw (at least for our purposes) being that is a word so many others already have a notion of, and, thus, a preconception about.

Therefore, in order to break away from these kinds of descriptions already soiled by conceptualization — much like the words "Verity" and "Vim" — we need to repurpose the language to more accurately describe the nuances of our understanding. For, what we are attempting to depict is the most important experience we can have as human beings. It is something we have all encountered, and yet, there is no real word for it in the English language. The kind of happening we are attempting to describe is a *being with*; the same "being with" we have alluded to up to this point. It is a joint action of the individual and Verity together; and that action gives great power to both the individual and Verity precisely because of the fact that Verity and the individual are merged through this happening which creates a kind of energy or Vim. *Being with* means that the individual can attune his or her consciousness or general being to a particular happening, and either observe that happening without the interference of conceptualization, or to act harmoniously *with* that happening. In other words, it is an action that either observes or interacts with a veritable occurrence, and, by doing so, creates a unique brand of Vim. *Being with* can take place at any time with any kind of consciousness; it is a type of experience that is obtained when conception has been cast away and replaced with an intimate awareness *of* a certain thing or a kind of communion or communication *with* that thing.

In the current construct of our consciousness, we as human beings do this business of communicating with Verity quite often; however, our largest difficulty is that we are unaware of it. Currently, the closest common description old language has of this experience is what it calls the act of "losing one's self". What is usually meant by this expression of "losing one's self" is that when we perform certain functions we become completely and totally immersed within the happening itself. This act can take almost every imaginable shape, from making love to watching television, to creating a work of art or talking with an old friend. When we fully and presently participate within the act, that happening is a kind of *being with*. It is a happening that both takes place wholly within the moment surrounded by and in the consciousness of the individual, while at the same time it calls forth a cosmic presence beyond the individual which is more so aligned with consciousness in its grand form. And, similarly, when we observe a veritable happening without attempting to interfere with it — whether we are looking at a mountain or watching our own breath enter and exit our body — that, too, is a kind of *being with*. And in this kind of happening there is no particular process to speak of; that is to say that there is nothing generally to work out, get to, or achieve; there is no actual seeking of a particular end — there is only the doing *of*, and, hence, only the *being with*.

In the unselfish, reciprocal relationship between the individual and Verity that causes a state of *being with*, there is only the doing or observing of the thing. And in that immersed brand of participation or observation, the individual and the happening become a singular process with no real delineation between act and actor, observer and observed. Again, this movement of the individual dancing harmoniously with the content of its consciousness or acting synchronistically with another veritable object is the process of *being with*. *Being with* is the original existential state. It is the kind of Being humanity supposedly possessed before having eaten from the Tree of Knowledge in The Garden of Eden. And in that state, much as the original biblical story indicated, there was no difficulty, no strife, and no suffering to speak of. The biblical description of human nature in its originality was indistinguishable from all other Being. For, when one possesses *being with* there is no thing within phenomena that can truly be deciphered as one or the other: both the individual and the thing exist harmoniously as one being or action. For, although our fragmented consciousness may see the apple as separate from the tree, in truth, neither could exist without the other. Which comes first is a trivial matter best left to the squabblings of pseudo-philosophers and the short-sighted arms of various scientific enclaves. What truly matters is not the first or the last, the whole or the part, but the meaning contained within all reality; and so long as conceptualization is the main implementation of consciousness, it is this meaning that will never be ascertained by the segmented thoughts espoused by various arms of the so-called prestigious academic branches. And again, what truly matters is only one's relationship to Verity and the subsequent meaning therein. For, *being with* is Verity merging with the individual and vice versa; and this pairing is the crux and ultimacy of all power, and with it the wisdom to further commune with reality and thereby comprehend the fact that, in the end, there is little to gain from the kind of knowledge given to Consciousness through conceptualization.

However, if we were to blend with Verity in earnest, this companionship would bring forth the paramount state of Consciousness and Being. Of course, what has been lost on us throughout the years is that this cohabitation is our natural conscious and existential state as human beings — as it is with all other beings as well. Never was an infant born who was so distracted by the concepts held within his of her mind that he or she was not totally attuned with their own simplistic minds and beings. And, likewise, there is no animal on the planet that has been taken so far down the path of conceptualization that it forgot what it was to live presently within itself at every moment. Yet, somewhere along the way, we, as grown human beings, lose this original connection to Verity. However, our war is the fight back to that very state. And yet, that is not to say that we hope to somehow lobotomize ourselves so that we forget all that we have learned. It's quite the opposite: at the conclusion of our war we should stand victoriously at a place where we are able to use concepts to help us achieve a *being with*. For, concepts can be used like soap: we can first wash ourselves with them, and we can then wash off that soap.

CORESCENCE

But we must also acknowledge the fact that modern language's toolkit currently does not have an accurate way to portray the happening which describes *being with*. Of course, how we speak about something affects the way we think about a certain thing, which, in turn, then helps dictate the experience we have with that thing. (We are, in fact, conceptualized.) Therefore, we need to again create a new term. Though, this time, however, our new term is an attempt to point to the experience of *being with*. Although, because we have almost no modern-day notion of this kind of experience — unlike our choices of "Verity" and "Vim" for their respective utilities — this term will be a word which has not yet been created by old language. We will, however, still honor the linguistic rules of old language and compose our word of roots that correspond to the various signifiers at play presently.

Taking all of this into consideration, the new word we have chosen in order to signify *being with* is *"corescence"*. Again, the etymological pillars of the word have not been chosen at random, but stay true to the current linguistic rules, with the root of "cor" meaning "with", and "esence" meaning "being"; therefore, the word quite literally means *being with*.[43] So, corescence — the *being with* — is the ultimate relational state between an individualized consciousness and veritable Being. It is an individual's harmonious immersion with Verity — whether Verity be an individual veritable occurrence or being, or an ultimate existential status; corescence is Verity and the individual in complete agreement and harmonious movement.

Though, here it becomes extremely important to understand that Verity is also something we hold within us. Verity is something that we can create just as much as it is something to be merged with. For, again, we must acknowledge the fact

---

[43] It is only that we have switched the prefix and suffix around, given that "esence-cor" simply has a rather awful tone to it both verbally and textually.

that corescence *is* our natural state of Consciousness and Being; it is a power that we not only *have*, but one that we *give*. And this ability to both connect with, only to be able to turn around and simultaneously create and then gift, should tell us something about not simply our relation to Verity, but what we really are as human beings. For, any being that can merge with, create, and then give Verity is also Verity itself. However, we are held back from this original capacity of ours through the invasion of our consciousness by conceptualization — which is, of course, why we have embarked on this war. But through corescence we become what we originally are and more. We not only come back to our true natures but attain a capacity for even further creativity and Vim.

THE INTIMATE RELATIONSHIP BETWEEN TIME & CONSCIOUSNESS

Here we must further recognize the intimate relationship between time, Verity, and Consciousness. As we have previously mentioned, when one engages in true corescence, time — as we have come to experience it — comes to a halt. Again, time is the playing field within Being on which Verity and Consciousness interact with one another, but it is also the product of that interaction. Verity is reality itself; but, like anything, that reality must be acknowledged in order to have existence in the first place. Of course, the kind of acknowledgment we speak of here is pure, unbiased recognition: it does not classify or qualify — for those tasks are left to the devices of conceptualization; the acknowledgement of an unbiased, deconceptualized consciousness simply observes and recognizes without interfering with Verity. And this observation *of* and subsequent interaction between various veritable objects and events produces time. For, time is the field where Consciousness is allowed to play itself out; which is also to say that time makes it possible for Consciousness to interact with Verity.

Yet, in corescence, time is unbounded by the rigor given to it through conceptualization; and, subsequently, the kind of linear time experienced through the limited capacities of human sensory perception takes on a different quality altogether. In truth, time is the connection and product between the self and Verity. Time is the expression of phenomena: it is the consequence of Being and Consciousness grappling with one another. In time, Verity unfolds, and we unfold along with it. However, in the linear sequence our consciousness has come to normalize, we see time as a movement *towards* something. Yet, if the linear progression was the true nature of time it would imply that time has an ultimate end or intention that it is heading towards, taking all of Being and experience along with it. This notion of time being inherently linear centralizes time as a prime factor in all of phenomena, when, in truth, time is more accurately the byproduct of the interactions of Being and Consciousness, and not the universal law which the scientific community (let alone our human consciousness as it is currently constructed) gives prominence to.

At base, the interactions of Being and Consciousness are merely various artful interplays of Vim interacting with itself within the grand scheme of Verity. All occurrence is Vim acting with, against, for, in, and through itself; all is Vim meeting Vim, creating Vim, killing Vim, but always there — in Verity and creating ever-more Verity as it goes along. And this pure action creates linear time in the way we experience it solely because of how our consciousness has come to construct itself, and not because sequential linear progression is time in its singular manifest. For, time, like Being, also needs something to observe *it*. And the way in which it is observed (or, more accurately, the capacities of the observer) will determine its apparent structure. And, again, as time is currently experienced through humanity's present conscientious construction, it is a *movement towards* and not necessarily the kind of *being with* we find in corescence.

Unarguably, time, in the linear sequence, appears to be going somewhere beyond its current location. However, this *movement towards* might just as well be described — much less, experienced — as a *movement from*. In fact, movements of any kind often suggest some sort of departure; and, being so, these movements are prone to be experienced as a means to a destination or a distinctive end, rather than eliciting a conscious recognition of a process that is meant to be experienced. Of course, in non-linear time (if we can imagine such a thing), it is the experience itself that is of central importance. Non-linear time is not beholden to anything but the interaction between Consciousness and its content. In non-linear time, events play out, but they do not necessarily do so in a sequence that can be traced from a "beginning" to an "end". That is, there is no "first", "next", or "last", precisely because *being with* eradicates the lineage of sequential time by shifting its *conscious focus* away from what comes *next* and fixating itself on what is *present*; rather, events take shape and unfold as they are experienced within the grand form of Consciousness, and then individualized consciousnesses themselves set up the parameters for their own content — and such content is not necessarily beholden to the temporality of the physical universe.

CONSCIOUSNESS &
THE PHYSICAL WORLD

Of course, we should note that the physical universe itself is merely shaped by the conscious capacities of the observer. As human beings we have physical bodies that are bound to the physical universe and its subsequent laws. Simply put, physical things relate to one another physically. Yet, physical beings, like all things, are determined by relationships. So, physical beings are determined by their relationships to other physical beings. However, the grand form of Consciousness is not merely physical, but also metaphysical. Therefore, in order to participate directly within the physical world, Consciousness needs a physical portal. For us as human beings, that physical portal is the brain. Of course, being made of physical matter, the brain is subject to the same kinds of laws and relationships as other physical objects. These relationships help to determine the brain's physical structure, and its physical structure helps elicit its conscientious capacities. What is remarkable, however, is that the conscientious capacities obtained by the brain can lead to a shift in the way the physical world is then experienced. The brain can evolve to pick up on certain physical happenings it was not previously able to detect, and this new detection changes the way it interacts with the physical universe, thus, augmenting that veritable relationship between the observer and the observed. The same thing happens in physical evolution: an organism takes a new form and alters the relationship it has with the world, thus, altering the world itself.

In a similar and possibly even more amazing capacity, the metaphysical activities of the brain can also augment the physical world by utilizing its metaphysical activities alone. Consciousness in both its grand and particularized forms can generate concepts and ideas that can go on to then alter the way the physical universe is interacted with. That is, a consciousness can create an idea about something and then use that idea to change its relationship with the physical world. For example, the idea that human beings could one day build a machine which would allow us to fly had to first be imagined. However, this idea was almost certainly given to the human consciousness initially by observing birds or other objects in the sky. So, once again, the linkage between Being and Consciousness proves itself to be inextricable.

Of course, purely conscious activity is not restricted to the laws set up within the realm of physical Being; again, this is easily demonstrated through the human capacity to imagine: in imagination all things become possible, and these possibilities are not restricted to the normal bounds given by dimensional space and linearly experienced time. However, the imagination is a kind of creative conceptualization, and, subsequently, only has a reality within a certain consciousness and only when that consciousness is fixated on that imagined idea. That is to say that imagined ideas or occurrences must be given direct and focused attention by an individual consciousness in order for them to have even the limited existence that such a consciousness is able to give to it. For, imagined ideas are not naturally upheld within the veritable physical world. For example, Mount Everest does not have to be imagined by a particular consciousness in order for it to exist; it already exists within the physical universe that is upheld by the grand form of Consciousness and Being; this being the case, Mount Everest does not need for a particular consciousness to focus on it in order for it to continue to exist. Whereas, Mount Sillymanjaro only has an existence in a child's mind as he pretends he is a mountaineer as he climbs up onto a couch; and the existence of this couch-mountain is obliterated as soon as the child loses focus on it. Obviously, the mere imagination of the child does not turn the couch into a veritable mountain. For, what is veritable has reality and truth independent of the recognition of a particular consciousness.

NON-LINEAR "TIME"

Verity and Consciousness need one another in order to exist, which means that there is no real difference between either supposedly independent entity. Furthermore, Verity exists in whatever way Consciousness allows, while at the same time, Consciousness is only able to perceive Verity in whatever way it exists. Yet, inextricably, the two form one another, and this formation of Consciousness and content creates time. However, here, by "time" what is really meant is more a "process" or a kind of general "happening" that is independent of time as a linear structure which moves towards or away from a fixed event. It is only when we give primacy to the *happening* and not to the *result* that we are able to detach ourselves from the notion of linear time and have an experience that is not only veritable, but is, in fact, much closer to the true constructs of time itself.

In corescence (the *being with* or merging of one's being or conscious with veritable reality), although time might exist, it does so on Consciousness's terms, not on the terms given via the parameters of physical space. Again, the non-linear time created within corescence allows for the event to unfold, granting its exclusive focus to the process rather than moving ahead towards an end which never truly arrives. Simply put, in corescence — or, the experience of *being with* — time exists as a tool so that a particular consciousness might interact with its content; whereas, in linear time, all events speed ahead and away from the moment regardless of the particular consciousness's ability to grasp it.

But corescence is the highest state of Being and Consciousness precisely because there is nowhere else to go; and in the state of corescence it is not that there has been something achieved, so to speak; but, more so, it is that there is nothing in particular to be done; for, in corescence, everything is already accomplished simply by participating with the happening. In linear time, however, the individual having the experience — along with all the Being and phenomena which surrounds the experiencer — are always being moved along. Within corescence, on the other hand, there is only a continuation of the being or the consciousness. And while new creativity might come out of that interaction, it is not necessarily at the mercy of linear time. For, true Consciousness is not hindered by the traditional parameters of time: Consciousness unfolds in its own way and in its own time; this is evidenced by any number of experiences we have on a daily basis — from how we come to experience time in our dreams to how we seem not to experience time at all when engaged in certain thoughts. It is not so much that our conscious operations are bound to time, but it is entirely more accurate to say that consciousness depends upon a particular being, and through that wokeness some kind of manifestation of time then grows up around it based upon how that consciousness has manifested or is able to play itself out. Again, this is readily experienced in dreams — where our minds often take us on journeys that span the course of a prolonged period in what is only a matter of minutes, or less, in the physical world. Of course, the pure-conscious experiences of our dreams seem just as real as those experiences we have in the physical world, yet they occur without the physical participation of our bodies.

To extend the lack of physical consciousness example to more extreme measures, those people whose physical bodies are incapacitated due to a prolonged state of physical unconsciousness (for example, a catatonic or comatose individual) do not experience the world in the same ways beings of normal cognition are able to. To the consciousnesses of those who are physically incapacitated, linear time is not a factor precisely because their ability to recognize it has been skewed. The same can be said of the sick or the segment of the population we might think of as mentally challenged, the elderly, the infantile — in fact, anyone who does not have a consciousness constructed in the ways we, as modern humanity have chosen to go about it, will have a different experience with time. Of course, undeniably, various beings within the physical world continue to interact with and influence one another and the beings and consciousnesses of ourselves as individuals, and those interactions continue to produce the linear, sequential time we have familiarized ourselves with. And while the effects of this sequential structure of time within Being are obvious given the fact that we appear to age with the progression of all the beings and events which surround our singular conscious vantage point, it is precisely because our vantage point is so singularly myopic that we cannot see the true, non-linear nature of time and Being.

INDIVIDUAL CONSCIOUSNESS IS LARGELY DETERMINED BEFORE BIRTH

Of course, how an individual has put its consciousness together is the real issue at hand. The kind of consciousness humans have allows for the kinds of beings we are, and the kinds of beings we are will dictate the kind of world we live in, and vice versa. Yet, the consciousness human beings have come to possess has not actually been selected by ourselves as individuals, but more so, our consciousness has been refined and handed down to us from generation to generation — as it is with the consciousness of all individualized beings.

If we are cognizant, we one day come to realize that we belong to a particular culture and nation, have a certain heritage or religion, live in an age that has a particular understanding of science, and that we speak a specific language that we use to describe our existential state — and that all of these things, through their various histories, do nothing short of dictate to us the general natures of our identities before we are able to actually come to any decision about our individual relationship to Verity. We are imprisoned by conceptualization before we become aware that we have a choice as to how we might be able to interact with the world. What's more is that if we are fortunate enough to realize that the kind of consciousness we have was shaped for us even before we were born, we are not able to break free from it by using the limited tools conceptualization has armed us with. So, even though we may attempt to coresce[44] and gain our own independent being by

---

[44] "Coresce" being the present tense verb of "corescence".

following our true natures, we cannot actually obtain Verity through conceptualization — which, again, given the way we have constructed our minds, is the only tool we actually have at our disposal.

As indicated previously, the "conscious" experiences of organisms without a central nervous system still do, however, have a kind of consciousness — although, it is clearly different from the experience of beings with nervous systems that also possess brains and the minds by which concepts can take root. Take, for example, any kind of gene within a living organism: a gene (or group of genes) produces a particular trait within its hosting organism. In fact, its primary function is to produce that particular trait. Naturally, its operation and programming come from its ancestry: similar genes in the ancestors of the gene's host organism were present, thrived, and were passed down to the next generation, allowing the current gene to inherit its operationality from those genes which came before it. Therefore, much like those beings with a conceptualized consciousness, the genes also have a predetermined mode of being passed down throughout the ages. It is only when they mutate that a change within the hosting organism occurs. Though, what is it that causes the gene (or any other organism) to behave in the way that it does? How does it know how to operate? And how is it able to both receive and pass that information along from and to its kin? In beings with nervous systems, the answer seems a bit more obvious given that where instinct (whatever instinct is)[45] falls short, an example of how

---

[45] Instinct may prove to be the most powerful ally we have in attempting to communicate the point that there is clearly a kind of unrecognized consciousness at play below the surface of Being.

to behave can be demonstrated from the parenting organism to its offspring.

But how is it possible for both living organisms without nervous systems and seemingly inanimate objects to pass on their traits to the following generation? The answer is clearly that these seemingly unconscious entities have an obvious awareness of both themselves and their surrounding given that they operate with a kind of intentionality usually reserved for the likes of what we might otherwise refer to as a "conscious being". In our example of the gene, that singular gene gives its host organism a very specific trait, and hence, has a precise and intentional function even though we do not necessarily think of a gene as 'conscious', per se. However, and again, what has Being has a kind of inherent awareness given that Being and Consciousness are one and the same (even though that awareness is not necessarily akin to the consciousness of beings containing a nervous system).

Again, all objects — whether animated or inanimate — have, at base, at least some kind of awareness of their own beings, if not an awareness of how their own beings interact with what stands immediately external to them. In order to exist, beings must either be aware of themselves or something must be aware of their particular being; even if that awareness is merely that such a being has physical attributes: for example, rocks are aware of themselves in that they are not attempting to be a tree or a knife or anything other than a rock. What's more is that the internal chemistry of the components that come to comprise the rock are aware that they function as something which holds together and forms a hardened physical mass; for these internal components that compose the rock, it is the *doing of* or the participation or *being with* that is the only consequence.

Nothing about the rock is debated or idealized: that which *is*, *does*; and by that pure action, the thing coresces and becomes one with Verity. Of course, there is no other choice: to act against Verity and not coresce would be to act against itself, and, in pure action (corescence) there is no choice — only the participation *with*.

VERITY CANNOT BE OBTAINED THROUGH CONCEPTION: ONE CAN ONLY EXIST ALONG WITH IT THROUGH CORESCENCE

Of course, the overwhelming difficulty is that Verity cannot be ascertained through conceptualization; yet, conceptualization is the primary means by which we attempt to relate to things in general. In an effort to "understand" a particular thing, we attempt to utilize the knowledge we have already obtained within our conceptual quiver. This is the essential problem with epistemology and science alike: both disciplines rely on their past laurels and achievements to obtain new horizons; therefore, essentially, a new paradigm is sought after through the washed-out utilities and resources of the old paradigm. We, as individuals, go through a similar process: if an attempt at a new comprehension is made in earnest, it is almost always done so by utilizing our conventional access points — which have become so commonplace to us we do not even see them as incapable or outdated. The conventional accesses are as seemingly banal as the language we use to describe a thing or our fundamental understanding about who we are as individual egos. However, depending on our reliance on conceptualization, these everyday utilities are potentially ill-equipped to allow us to truly coresce with and fully comprehend any new experiences that might present themselves to us. Simply stated, we are so set in our ways that there are very few occasions to actually have a new experience — to actually coresce to a point where the observer and the observed (the consciousness and its content) become one and the same being.

Verity — which is obtainable only through this process of corescence — is not something to be understood: it is something to be acted and participated *with*. This is why we describe the process of corescence as a *being with*. The irony, however, is that the natural state of *all* Being is one of corescence; this is so given that Being is birthed by and through Vim and Verity; therefore, Being emanates from Verity and enjoys a natural harmony with it. It is only through conceptualization that this natural linkage is severed; this being the case, we must further understand our own beings and our own consciousness as having a deeply intimate linkage to that veritable source of all things. Indeed, Verity is what we are! And, given this truth, we need to comprehend our own abilities and capacities as stewards of that ultimacy. Although, in our attempts at comprehending things in general, we often make an initial misstep; for, in that general attempt at comprehension we almost always employ our cerebral capacities alone. And, once again, being that our cognition is frequently misrouted by the various concepts it employs, attempting to fully comprehend any given thing by using the sole utility of our minds is almost always a sure-fire way to misinterpret phenomena. Therefore, we must go beyond the limited capacity of our consciousness and seek out a more holistic process which brings us back into that natural state of corescence from which we originally came.

We must, quite literally, *be with* that which we are attempting to gain access to if we ever hope to gain access to it in the first place! Yet, this can only be done through action alone. For, in the act there is a blending of being between the action and the actor. As it is when the observer becomes the observed, in the purity of action, the distinguishment between deed and doer forge into one happening and the actor becomes the act and vice versa; for, just as it is with all interplays of Vim and Verity, each being needs the other in order to exist, and, in reality, there is no actual difference between one and the other.

In deeper examination, one may come to recognize that the act itself is the very essence, catalyst, and meaning of Being. For, in the act we find not only direction but also purpose. And if we were to search deeply into the existence of purpose, we may well find that it is purpose itself that drives a form out of nothingness and into Being. However, none of this can be discovered through the process of conceptualization alone; the act must play itself out, and the actor must have a certain level of corescence with that action in order to take away a sense of purpose from it. For it is only when we are participants *with* that Verity avails itself; and to participate *with* means that the entirety of one's being must be immersed in the action. However, using conceptualization alone we can never truly coresce, but, at the very most, might only sojourn through Verity's dwelling.

THE LINEAR PRESENTATION OF TIME WITHIN CONSCIOUSNESS

Living or being *with* — through doing or engaging in the thing itself — is the only way to have an experience capable of profoundly influencing the experiencer. And this brand of experience is one that happens outside of the conventional parameters of time and space precisely because of the ways in which it impacts the individual consciousness. Here, again, we should be reminded that time, like all things, is a construction of the particular consciousness. That events appear to unfold in a linear sequence is merely a tool which a consciousness utilizes in order to be able to apprehend the event fully; by seeing the event unfold sequence by sequence, a particular consciousness can pay close attention to the individual occurrences within the event, as if those individual occurrences were singular frames of a video file or film reel. So, events within phenomena present themselves to our consciousness (in the way it is currently organized) as a process which is unpacked through a linear sequence; this linear sequence unfolds as such so that consciousness is able to apprehend the event both through its various stages and as a whole. So, by sequencing the events, a particular consciousness is able to unpack phenomena and track its evolution; that is, by stringing the event together piece by piece, a consciousness can utilize the tool of sequential time to *be with* each individual occurrence within that event, moment by moment. And when a particular consciousness is fully opened, creative, and attuned, corescence occurs and the whole of that experience interacts with that consciousness in such a way that each becomes a part of the other: the experience is held within the individual's consciousness, which allows that consciousness to expand while simultaneously ensuring that the event is able to continue to unfold within that particular consciousness. And within the totality of that act, both the phenomenological event and the particular consciousness are given a rejuvenated life which permits each to creatively expand into novel modes of consciousness and new events in a perpetual cycle.

EXPERIENCE AS THE TRUE PROCESS

However, even though the experience stays within the individual's consciousness it does not necessarily come to hinder the individual's ability to have new experiences; this is not the case with conception, however. In conception, once a concept is forged that notion then goes on to inform and influence the experiences which follow it. Whereas, the experiences gained through corescence actually expose the individual consciousness to Verity in new and different ways that open up the possibility for further creativity. So, even though a corescent experience might stay with an individual, that individual becomes more creative and open to still further creativity through drawing upon that corescent experience. In this way, corescence is the exercise of limbering up one's general conscious experience so that it might be more open to other experiences — experiences which then continue that process in a cyclical fashion. Conception, however, has the opposite effect on a mind: the more conceptions a particular mind holds, the more rigidly it has to abide to those notions and the beliefs they produce. However, through its own creative capacities, corescence grants its participant the ability to both "have" and simultaneously "let go of" other experiences. (Although, the exact meaning of possession in this case is slightly different than we would otherwise think of it.)[46]

But it is exactly in this process that time as we have come to understand it through conception becomes altogether unreal: experience is the only true process; time is merely its byproduct. Whatever is gleaned from experience is unbounded by time's apparently linear sequence. And when we are corescing, that experience is one we both take with us through all other experiences, but simultaneously opens us up to the possibilities of new experiences precisely because that corescent experience has transcended us by unlocking a new potential within us. And it is exactly this potential that dictates the kind of consciousness we possess. Of course, in reality, consciousness is not in any way actually beholden to the linear progression of time. This is another meaning of corescence: to bring both the thing to us and us to the thing and to have both be altered and meld into one another because of that interaction — which then continues ceaselessly without end, given that one now fundamentally comprises the other. This is the ending of conventional time and the conjuring of a force that is both apart from, yet simultaneously with us in all of our doings. For, action is all that there is. All is action within action. All is Vim through Vim.

---

[46] This is a prime example of conceptualization in language failing us: the meanings of the words "have" and "let go of" are historically used to signify a certain kind of occurrence within phenomena. However, the kind of occurrence we are attempting to describe here falls short of the traditional utility of the words, so we must use the words while at the same time deconstructing them.

BEYOND "COMPREHENSION"

Attempting to engage with various forms of Being or events through the sole use of one's cerebral abilities alone does an injustice to the capacity of human nature. This effort to codify phenomena into conceptual laws is the laziest way to interact with Being. So, in order to pave the pathway to corescence and thereby bypass the purely cerebral operations of conceptualization, we need to recognize the inextricable ties we have to Verity within our own selves.

And this recognition involves the realization that we belong not just to ourselves as individuals, but to a shared *condition* of humanness. In truth, by living out our human condition we are responsible for the entirety *of* that condition. And if we were to reorient our current outlook so that we understood ourselves as intimately connected to the many forms which comprise our beings, the seemingly smaller actions of our lives might not seem so inconsequential.

So, the question which then arises is how do we go about comprehending our own beings? Up to this point we have generally used the methodology of concepts to digest our existential state. Yet, existence itself is done with the entirety of our beings. That is, existence is something that, although conceived of through consciousness, also goes beyond it. So, it makes for both good sense and practice that the process of comprehension is a task not given to our minds alone. In fact, although it may seem like an absurd statement given our current understanding of comprehension *as* a process, it is nevertheless one of the hopes of our war that we transform that entire process of what we currently understand as "thought" into an activity that is beyond the mere capacity of the mind; that is to say that one of our war's objectives is to move the process of "thinking" to something that is beyond the limited capacities of a cerebral happening and into the presence of a *being with* that is experienced by the whole of our abilities and not just the capacities of our minds alone. Of course, in reality, there is nothing that actually needs to be achieved in order for this process to begin: this kind of holistic ability to comprehend and experience with the entirety of our beings is our natural human state within Being; for, Being, by its very nature, is that which interacts with Verity *as* a process; of course, Being is able to have this interaction with Verity without the hampering of a "mind" as we have come to cultivate it. The capacity to go beyond the mind in order to "think" is already there; we merely need to flush it out by deconstructing (or unlearning) our current conscious modality.

VERITY'S ULTIMATE FREEDOM & INABILITY TO BE OBTAINED

Similarly, there is nothing we need to necessarily do in order to comprehend or achieve Verity. In fact, Verity is not achievable: for, Verity *is*, and, being so, *is* already. (Therefore, achievement is moot being that the aspiration is already accomplished.) Similarly, there is nothing that needs to be done to understand Verity; again, the only thing which needs doing is to unlearn conceptualization as a process, or, at the very least, unlearn the methods which give conceptualization the primacy by which we go about consciously interacting with and within phenomena. This is Verity's secret and its promise: that it is there, and it is there already and everlasting. Verity is the actual, the real — the voice and song of Being. It is the hand of time and the cradle of all phenomena itself; and we are intimate players within it. Verity is the all-encompassing presence; and while Vim's many forms play out within it in all manners of ways, it is Verity that is the common thread. And, again, it is exactly because of this omnipresence that there is nothing which needs attaining or achieving. That which needs attaining or achieving is done so through effort, but no effort is required to coresce with Verity. And precisely because there is no need to shore up any kind of connection, this effortless relation gives the gift (and potential curse) of ultimate freedom. For, given that there is nothing to attain we are left only with the capacity to work with Vim in whatever ways we so choose.

While Verity is the road, Vim is the carriage; and how we operate it is to our discretion. Yet, to operate this carriage efficiently we need to have a clear understanding of what *is*. Because the ultimate freedom we've been given through Verity can be a dangerous weapon if the consciousness which implements it is clouded. And while Verity is choiceless, the immense freedom it allows for is full of decision at every step. This is Verity's singular difficulty: there can be no true freedom without boundless choice. Yet, boundless choice can be one's undoing — especially if a particular consciousness is not given the pretext.

So, the paradoxical reality arises: how can one be free without the choice to enslave one's self? Uncoincidentally, if one is truly aligned with Verity then the potential for self-enslavement is significantly less than it would be otherwise.

Of course, in true alignment with Verity, choices become clear: one follows Verity, or one does not. To follow Verity eventually always leads to Vim and the state of life and consciousness therein. Therefore, such a choice is often quite literally a matter of life or death. By following Verity, we link arm and arm with its handmaiden in Vim and further all that which is active and creative; and this creativity helps not only our own beings to progress, but all Being and Consciousness along with it. Essentially, the partnership we form with Vim is the only thing of true significance. It is that partnership which stokes the embers of potential within all Being — and such potential can only truly be realized if we are forever pushing into that creative frontier, and thereby expanding the realm of Verity by doing so.

Vim's natural plight is one of progression through creativity. So, Vim's disciples merely follow that organic movement *into*, and such a movement assembles new relationships and creates new kinds of beings and events as it carves its way in and through phenomena. However, its direction is not necessarily a movement towards something so that it might obtain a certain status, objective, or particular thing; more so, the movement and natural creativity which come from it *is* the purpose and the reward. What Vim moves "into" or "through" is of little consequence — as Vim's course is, by its very nature, *the* course, and *the* course is the one which all Consciousness ultimately seeks; so, again, there is nothing one needs to do in order to coresce but to follow Vim's organic movements — which, ironically enough, are also one's own movements; for, as we have already noted: Vim, Verity, and Consciousness are all one and the same.

And yet, within the unobstructed ranges of ultimate freedom, the act of following can be a difficult thing to do. The question is: are we implementing and following Vim, or have we chosen a path which gives us the illusion of a kind of power that usurps it?

EATING THE ROTTEN FRUIT FROM THE TREE OF KNOWLEDGE IN AN ATTEMPT TO GAIN INSTANT KNOWLEDGE & FREEDOM

Our current human condition demands that we dwell under the shade of that ancient Tree of Knowledge and not so much eat from its branches but scour the ground in search of its fallen fruits, now rotting in the muck. For it is not so much that humanity itself is fallen, but it is more so that our access to knowledge currently lies a great deal lower than it once did: and again, it is not so much that humanity picks the low-hanging fruit of knowledge, but it is far more accurate to say that the fruit itself has fallen off the vine and become rotten. (And what bitter tastes it has!)

Of course, the knowledge we gain from eating these fruits is only that: it is only knowledge alone, hollow and without context. Such empty knowledge lacks the true perspective and relation to Verity that is only forged through experience. But humanity has made the same continuous blunder since its inception: we are tempted to pass over experience in exchange for an attempt at instant enlightenment — however unearned it might be. We wish for wisdom without the work.

But are we willing to suffer our way to truth through experience and *being with*? Or do we prefer to gain the direct knowledge *of*, and forego the difficulties embedded within the road of experience? One is the path of Vim. The other is the lofty, though unrealistic pursuit of a freedom which we hope will ultimately empower us, yet, in actuality, leads us to nowhere other than the prison-blocks of conceptualization.

If we see clearly, such a choice becomes so obvious that it is hardly a choice at all. Yet, in an ultimate paradox, in order to have the fullest understanding possible, we often need to choose against the obvious pathway laid out by Vim and go our own way — a way which may very well run counter to Verity. The danger becomes real, however, when we realize that choosing freedom often means that there is nothing on which to fall back. For, in true and ultimate freedom, one blazes one's own trail, and in doing so may cut a pathway too deep into the wilderness to find an easy way out. Because we must realize that in ultimate freedom there is only the self. And if it is not properly structured, the ultimately free self is capable of doing a great deal of harm to everything it encounters.

THE BONDS OF FREEDOM

Although, given this perspective on ultimate freedom, maybe it was not so much that original humanity was expelled from The Garden, but more so that they chose to leave it in hopes of discovering a new *brand* of freedom; and once this new freedom was discovered it was simultaneously realized that there was no escaping it. After all, although freedom promises the potential of all things, in reality, unchecked freedom is little more than a mirage in an inveritable wasteland. And here, outside of the shades of The Garden, there is only the blistering sun of freedom in every direction. And we walk through that openness — a desert of freedom where, ironically, the only potential which thrives is that of death.

Such is the world without a proper attachment to reality: it is a moonscape of lofty ideals and unrealistic hope, all set up by the rationale that somehow freedom — whatever that is — will deliver us. But it is just another ruse in the bottomless bag of conception's foul tricks: for the notion of freedom is as alluring as any of its other deceits.

However, what freedom really is is not what the common notion purports it to be. For there can be no actual freedom if the ground of Verity is not properly set underfoot. Somewhat paradoxically, however, there can be no full attainment of Verity unless we first walk out of that garden under the delusion of our freedoms only to realize that Verity was never anything to be obtained until we began searching for it. And through this search that was initially spawn by a want for freedom and the illusory powers it supposedly holds, the human consciousness has complicated its reality: through a *chosen* outlook, humanity has wandered away from the simplicity of its natural relationship to Verity and abandoned basic corescence in favor of an approach which attempts to abstract all Being through muddied cerebral comprehensions. And this quest is unwritten by a further abstracted notion of "freedom" and the knowledge it allegedly grants to those who seek it.

CONSCIOUSNESS'S MANUFACTURED DUALISM IN ATTEMPTING TO RELATE TO BEING

Some proclaim humanity to be "fallen". Others have declared the death of God. Both are conceptions. For things are not "this" or "that"; they merely *are*. To proclaim something as located in one place or another — as having one quality or another — sets up a relation that tells only a partial story. But we, through our war, are fighting to liberate Consciousness from the dualism it has produced in attempting to relate to Being.

But it is a war we must fight, and it is one we must fight in this way; because, as it were, we could not re-enter The Garden and understand its true meaning without having first left its confines. For, through our departure from that veritable garden, we continue to create and redouble Verity. And no matter where we are located, we are still Verity's kin. But we must further recognize that we are also Verity's agents, and this carries with it a grave responsibility. For, if we realize our role within Verity itself, we will clearly see that our existence is vital to Verity's own. We have the capacity to empower and compel the true power of all Being. And what's more: we, ourselves, have the power to create Being and also *to be*.

CONSCIOUSNESS IS THE CONTAINER OF BEING & BEING ALLOWS FOR CONSCIOUSNESS

In Verity, there is only what is. And what *is* could not *be* if there were nothing there to observe it. For Being alone cannot support itself; it needs a container, and that container is Consciousness. And within that container all things are there and, if properly structured, all potentials are allowable — which is to say that all things are able to realize their ultimate freedoms. Just as so, all things likewise participate in that grand happening; and this is the glory and the horror of Being. It is its song and its secret: that Being and Consciousness are one movement — one operation that interacts with itself, communicates with itself, creates itself, and even ingests and destroys itself. But it is all Vim interacting with Vim, trading form for nothingness and nothingness for form and creating anew.

And in that reality is the great comfort: for there is no ending to Verity; there is only the recreation of various forms of Vim. Verity, however, is eternal. And we are a part of that eternality. And Verity's action is the perception and communication of and with itself: it is perception of perception — a hall of mirrors, and in each reflection a new perspective of the same veritability. And Consciousness, in its collectivity, is, at base, the same as the consciousness that emanates from the singular perspective. The conscious of one is the Consciousness of all; it is both king and servant simultaneously.

So, again, our challenge now becomes one of implementation: how do we shape this awesome responsibility? For, consciousness evolves by looking at and working with itself. So, our actions are of enormous consequence. The consciousness we have *is* the freedom; it is the living representation of our move away from The Garden of Verity. And it is of no small irony that through this crusade we have become cognizant of the fact that Consciousness itself is the battlefield upon which this war rages.

ALL IS PRESENT

Again, in Verity, there is only what *is*. Verity is something we are not bonded *to*, but something that we already *are*. And if we realize our innate natures, at the same time we see that — precisely because Verity already *is* and we are a part of that being — there is no need to *become*. To be in accordance with Verity there is nothing to gain — only that which we must lose. What *is* is already present; it is only a matter of concocting that inner alchemy. There are no ready-to-hand tools we must implement; we are the tool of Verity, and Vim is *our* tool to cultivate.

Once Verity is fully within our consciousness — once it is a part of everything we do, once we are truly *with* — we see that there is no need for an intermediary of any sort. Likewise, Verity abolishes the absolute need for systems, institutions, traditions, and the general reliance on prescriptions or patterns of any kind. For Verity is there already; and no pathway or ideology is needed in order to bring it forth.

Verity is a presence that is as deific as it is human. It is something we can communicate not only *to*, but *with*. And in that communication *with* lies the secret of *being with*. For all action is a form of communication; and if we bring a conscious awareness into those acts, our entire being — along with consciousness itself — is elevated.

Yet, strangely enough, in this conscientious movement of communicating and being *with*, although consciousness is given a new plane on which to exist, at the same time Verity is something that we obtain more so through an interactive feeling than through an isolated cerebral thought. And all motivation arises for the sake of a feeling. Even those acts which are purely cerebral (thoughts) are only then acted upon because of the feelings they produce. Indeed, all Being itself is a feeling. All Being is connected through its proverbial heart. And if we feel it beating it will carry us at every moment and give us life just as we give a life to it. Again, this is its power as well as ours: we are inextricably connected to the unrelenting powers of all creation. And our significance is tied up solely in our realization of those powers; therefore, all we need to do is recognize that significance and act upon that realization.

For, we do have freedom, but it is not as it is traditionally described: our freedom is contingent upon our recognition of Verity and our relationship to *it*, and not to the abstract notion of freedom itself. For true freedom is creative and empowering — just as we would expect any truly veritable thing to be. But in that freedom we have only greater responsibility: for our choices create our reality and influence Verity and Vim themselves, just as what they are influences us. So, to steer human consciousness off course by distracting it with abstractions is the only way in which conceptualization can survive. And if conceptualization cannot survive, it seeks to kill the mind of humanity along with it.

And how will it go about this attack?

It cannot attack Verity directly — for Verity already *is*, and being so, is ultimately indestructible. But it *can* attack a third of its trinity by infiltrating Consciousness, mortally wounding it, and then, like a cancer, overwhelming it.

So, we must understand that this war is the greatest war because it is a struggle not for the existence of a race of people or a country or a way of life, but it is a struggle for existence itself. It is a battle for the structure of Consciousness and how it ultimately operates. Life is a gift, and we are its stewards. Yet we act as though we are at the mercy of this life — as though we are so often somehow the victims *of* it, and not blessings *to* it. We serve as batteries to conceptualization — hosts of ideological parasites — and wait to be saved, or at the very least distracted. But Verity can be both our soul's savior and the occupant of our conscious if we allow for it. For when at long last we come to the realization that we are the truth and the very power and essence of this world itself, we will finally acknowledge, once and for all, our own importance in the hierarchy of Being, and come to know and understand that we are royal; and it is a bloodline given to us by our direct descendent in Verity. We are more than ourselves — just as all things are more than themselves because of Verity.

Verity is the final thing, the real thing, the only thing; and it is the thing we have been looking for without being able to name it exactly. And we have to keep it, name it, and interact with it; and by doing so we then realize, with our conceptual minds, that the importance of naming and calling out to it gives us a power greater than any we could have otherwise ever known or imagined. Because it is not a power meant to be possessed or dominated by one: it is a power shared, and because of this symbiotic and reciprocal relation, it is a power so great that to attempt to direct it actually detracts from it. And we are better off riding the strengths of its currents, anyhow. For, to harness Vim is to ride a dragon. We have to watch our thoughts and actions and rid Consciousness of those intentions born purely of conception — almost all of which seek to serve the lone individual. For, at our basic states we are all connected by Verity. And Verity does away with all conception and the dualism which springs from it.

Verity *is*. Verity *does*. And we will need it to win the greatest war humanity has ever known. If we keep it close there is no possibility of defeat. Though, if we trade it in for any number of conceptualization's substitutes, there is no possibility of victory.

So, here and now the stage is set. The battle lines are drawn. Enemies and allies are clear. Our objective is known. There is nothing left to do but fight. And fight we will.

After all, there is no alternative to victory.

For, Verity is......And so are we ......